Witchcraft

This book includes:

Witchcraft for beginners, Moon Spells, Herbal Magic, Cristal Magic. Learn Rituals and Spells of Wicca Religion. A guide for modern Wiccan.

Text Copyright © Linda Candles

Legal & Disclaimer

The information contained in this book and its contents is not designed to replace or take the place of any form of medical or professional advice; and is not meant to replace the need for independent medical, financial, legal or other professional advice or services, as may be required. The content and information in this book have been provided for educational and entertainment purposes only.

The content and information contained in this book has been compiled from sources deemed reliable, and it is accurate to the best of the Author's knowledge, information and belief. However, the Author cannot guarantee its accuracy and validity and cannot be held liable for any errors and/or omissions. Further, changes are periodically made to this book as and when needed. Where appropriate and/or necessary, you must consult a professional (including but not limited to your doctor, attorney, financial advisor or such other professional advisor) before using any of the suggested remedies, techniques, or information in this book.

Upon using the contents and information contained in this book, you agree to hold harmless the Author from and against any damages, costs, and expenses, including any legal fees potentially resulting from the application of any of the information provided by this book. This disclaimer applies to any loss, damages or injury caused by the use and application, whether directly or indirectly, of any advice or information

Table of Contents

Witchcraft for Beginners

Witchcraft Moon Spells

Witchcraft for Beginners

A modern guide for modern Wiccan. Understand the mysteries of Witchcraft and Wicca Religion and learn Magic Rituals with Spells, Herbal Magic, Crystal Magic and Candles.

Linda Candles

Book Description

How many religions or religious beliefs can you count on one hand? My guess would be that the fingers on one arm could not come close to the real answer. Further, I highly doubt Wicca would be in your list of five (the list would go something like Christianity...Islam...Buddhism...). To some end, Wicca is a form of paganism. The word Wicca literally translates to 'witch' in Old English. Remember when we talked about religious beliefs being old?

Wicca is one of the oldest religions known to man. If you are a keen history buff, you will know that man has practiced magic for as far back as he was able to communicate; with himself and a higher power. Being one of the oldest religions, you are probably also wondering why it is not as popular as Christianity or Islam. I have no concrete answer for you. However, I would speculate and say that part of the reason is that over the decades, the practice has had its fair share of myths especially because of its relation to witchcraft, (Wicca is the preferred tittle to witch because witchcraft has a dark past and negative connotation).

Unlike most religions and religious beliefs that demand complete unwavering devotion, Wicca can co-exist with your scientific outlook and religious beliefs. Many Wiccans with a firm understanding of its teachings will tell you that Wicca provides a means by which you can understand the mysteries of life from a different perspective; a perspective that embraces the two energy forces of the world (feminine and masculine). With this explanation fresh in your mind, let me tell you that you can use Wicca to transform your life. Are you surprised? It is true that you can actually use the essential, rooted wisdom of Wicca to make modern life better. Before we get to that bit, let us roll back time, and take a glimpse of the rich history of Wicca.

This book gives a comprehensive guide on the following:

- A brief history of Wicca and its relation to today
- Witchcraft
- Intermediate Wicca
- Advanced Wicca
- Wicca: Book(s) of Shadows
- Wicca and Magic
- Tools of wiccan ritual: the athame
- Wiccan clothing and ritual attire
- Wicca Goddess and Gods
- Sabbats and esbats
- Healing spells
- Divination spells... AND MORE!!!

Introduction

The word Wicca originates from the Old English and means simply, "witch." Older Germanic languages attribute additional meanings such as foretell, speak, and divine (as in divination).

But what does a witch do? We may have been taught to connect witchcraft with darker things such as evil, Satanism, and manipulation, but only the last word is correct. A witch does manipulate things but only within themselves. Then, we resonate the effects of that change outward into the world.

There are many forms of modern Pagan practice; Wicca is one of them.

The birth of Wicca as a modern religion can be traced back to the writings of a retired British civil servant, Gerald Gardner—in fact; there is an entire branch of Wiccan practice devoted to him called Gardnerian Wicca. He published his definitive book on the subject, Witchcraft Today back in 1954. Gardner also founded a coven—essentially a prayer/workgroup for witches, numbering anywhere from four to 40 members or more—and several members of his coven went on to publish books on the subject of witchcraft and magical living.

In Gardnerian and other traditional practices, a coven is led by a priest and priestess, who oversee the ceremonial Sabbath rituals and often represent the god and goddess during these rituals. They are also in charge of educating newer members of the coven and helping members move upward in the steps of a witch's formal education and life—wiccaning (naming), handfasting, croning, etc.

Chapter 1 A brief history of Wicca and its relation to today

If you ask ten Wiccans about their religion, you will get ten conflicting answers or even more. In my view, this is only a walking distance from the truth. Part of the reason for this disparity is that tens of thousands of Americans practice Wicca (the number is still not definitive). What then compounds this is the fact that there are some several thousand different Wicca groups all practicing a different form of the religion (sort of like the different branches of Christianity. Catholics... Presbyterian etc.). Further, Wicca as a religion has no governing body and no religious book. Wicca and its practice today vary greatly from one tradition to the other. However, a few ideals and beliefs have stood the test of time. They form a common trait with all modern practices of Wicca.

There is a lot of misinformation about the origin of Wicca as a religion. Let me dispel this. Gerald Gardner introduced Wicca, the religion, in the 1950s. In the beginning, the practice was secretive, initiatory, and oath bound. A few years after its first introduction, splinter cells formed with new and liberal traditions. However, even today, most of the splinter cells follow the principles first introduced by Gardener. There is reason to believe that Wicca is not a traditional religious belief.

However, Gardner did use some old esoteric knowledge to build his principles. This includes Kabballah, Eastern mysticism and some British Legend.

Today, Wiccans are your next-door neighbor, your doctor, your kid's teacher, soccer moms and so many more. In simple terms, it means that a Wiccan could be anyone. Unlike Christians who outwardly proclaim their faith and try to convert others to the religion, Wiccans have no desire to become 'fishers of men'. Because the religion is not always on a recruitment drive, some mystery about it still abounds. Let us go back a bit to Gardner and his practice of Wicca because it forms a great part of the practice of Wicca today.

Although Wicca (witchcraft) is an old practice, the practice of Wicca gained popularity through Gardner. History has it that the Gardner was initiated into a coven, the New Forest Coven in the 1930s. His form of Wicca practice was the Gardnerian tradition. Since then, the practice of Wicca has boomed partly due to the fact that in the 1970s, many publishers such as Paul Huson, Janet Farrar, Scott Cunningham and many more advocated for self-initiation into the craft. The rise in popularity of the practice meant that it gained partially popularity amongst the young, hip crowd because of its integration into TV shows and films.

I also have to state and point out that Wicca, the Wicca we know today, has its building blocks in the early 16th and 17th century. Again, if you are a history buff, you know that during this era, many people died due to what was then known as "witch hunts". Since then, science has proven that there was no justification for these killings and that the 'witches' did not have any form of religious practices. Those who practiced Wicca in the early days believed it to be a continuation of the practices of these 'witches'.

Wicca does not preach, practice, or embrace the concepts of heaven and hell, sin, confessions, the evils of nudity or sex, animal sacrifices, Satanism, or the inferiority of a woman. Further, the Wicca in practice today is not a fashion statement, nor is it a lifestyle or way of dressing.

In addition to the above, I should also point out that initiation and a degree system is a common practice in most modern Wicca covens. In these covens, initiation serves the symbolic purpose of a rebirth by which the initiate dedicates him or herself to the gods of the Wiccan tradition. Further, most of these covens have the common practice and belief that only a person who has reached the level of Third degree dedicant may act as a high priest or priestess. All Wiccans acknowledge the polarity of the Divine, which honors both male and female deities. Moreover, a Wiccan may opt to honor a specific god or goddess or choose to honor a non-specific god or goddess. Wicca has many deities, some of which are Osiris, Athena, Herne, Belsis, and Apollo. In the Gardnerian practice of Wicca, the name of the gods and deities are a guarded secret only known to initiated members.

As stated earlier, despite its branching off, some principles remain constant with each coven. One of these beliefs is the use of spell work and magic. We can attribute this to the Wiccan belief that magic has no supernatural trait. It is simply the harnessing and redirection of energies all around us. A Wiccan can then use this energy to effect change in the environment and the world around us. To Wiccans, magic and spells are simply tools or skills. However, most Wiccans do use specific tools while spell crafting. Some of the more common tools are Athame, herbs, candles, crystals, and wand. Further, most of the magic and spelling occurs within a spell circle and the use of magic is not restricted to the high priests and priestesses: with a bit of practice anyone can spell.

To some degree, most Wiccans accept the concept of an afterlife. Therefore, most Wiccans accept the concept of interacting with the spirit world and contact with the unknown (read spirit world) is not unheard of.

In the next section, for posterity, we shall look at the different arms/types of Wicca in practice today and since recorded history of the practice of Wicca What is Witchcraft?

Witch craft is the belief and even practice in magical skills that are either exercises by an individual or a group of people. It is often believed that witch craft is a complex concept that is going to very between societies and cultures.

However, when using the term witch craft should be used with caution depending on which culture you're talking about because it is not a cross-cultural term that means the same thing in each culture.

Witch craft often plays a religious or medicinal role when it comes to societies or groups that believe in magic.

However, witch craft can actually share a common ground when it comes to things such as sorcery, magical, superstition, paranormal, necromancy, shamanism, healing, possession, spiritualism, occult, and even nature worship.

Chapter 2 Witchcraft

Now that we have covered all the basics of Wiccan beliefs, we must go into one of the most common practices and that is witchcraft. Witchcraft is probably the most widely misunderstood practice and Wiccans are forced to deal with the stigma and judgment that comes along with practicing witchcraft. This is ironic because the sole purpose of the practice is to help, heal and project good into the world. At least that is what most Wiccans believe because we adhere to the Rule of Threefold and the quote from the Rede "An it harms none, do what ye will". Whether you choose to practice witchcraft for good or for bad, you must know the basics so that you can make informed decisions.

Witchcraft's Historical Place in Society

It is important to understand the term witchcraft and its background in society. Anthropology has almost always defined the term in a negative way. This is where the evil witch stigma and myth comes from. Anthropologists have commonly defined witchcraft as the "conscious intent of causing harm." They say that witches would use rituals, magic, spells and manipulate substances such as herbs in order to assassinate political powers, harm innocent civilians and hurt their enemies.

What needs to be understood here is that there is a major difference between what people have said witches were doing and what they were actually practicing.

You see, we get our historical evidence mostly from Christian sources. This is because Christians were the most highly educated groups of people and pagans, heathens or other people living on the fringes were not usually the ones writing books. Therefore, we must take any accounts of witches or witchcraft written by those historians with a grain of salt.

We know that during the witch trials, Christians burned witches at the stake and justified these actions by saying they were evil Satan worshippers who sacrificed babies and poisoned the town's water supply. It wouldn't look very good on Christianity if they were burning people simply because they were pagans and lived an alternative lifestyle, although that is probably exactly what happened.

Living a life that was not Christian meant that these pagans were not falling under Christian power and that didn't sit well with them. Christians have historically done this to many groups of people who have not abided by their religion. They have also persecuted Jews, Muslims and lepers and simply used them as a scapegoat. Although it will likely never be historically proven, the chances of witches being used as a scapegoat by Christians rather than practicing evil are very high - in my opinion.

As we know from earlier in this book, Margaret Murray was the first prominent historian to write about how the witches burned at the stake were not evil Satan worshippers but were practicing a pre Christian religion, called witchcraft.

Before we go further, I feel it is my duty to remind you that many historians have discredited and disagreed with Murray and her theories on witches, meaning that we probably will never know the truth about pre-Christian pagan rituals and practitioners of witchcraft. That being said, we **do** know what Gerald Gardner had in mind when he was establishing the modern practices, we observe in Wicca today.

Wicca and Witchcraft

Gerald Gardner accepted Murray's theory wholeheartedly and based all his beliefs and traditions around what we can call a **historical** definition of witchcraft. This definition removes all negative connotation and association with evil or Satan and is simply the **exercise or invocation of supernatural powers to control people, environments or events.** Many Wiccans will take this definition and broaden it even further, stating that witchcraft is **any use of tools, substances or spells in order to invoke change in someone's health, state of mind, or environment.** This definition would include the use of aromatherapy and herbalism as part of witchcraft.

Remember that Wicca doesn't have any hard and fast rules so the definition of witchcraft is completely up to you. You can decide whether or not you believe in certain practices and whether or not you choose to partake in them. This means that you can absolutely be a Wiccan but not necessarily practice witchcraft or magic.

Witchcraft is also an umbrella term for rituals, incantations, practices, and traditions so you could be a witch, practicing witchcraft but not believe in the Wiccan deities or other beliefs. This would make you a witch, but not a Wiccan. It should also be noted that the word "witch" describes both male and female practitioners of witchcraft. Warlocks are male witches who practice evil magic. They are seen as traders of the craft and are looked down upon by white or "good" witches, which I will go out on a limb and say are the majority of witches.

To make things a little more complicated, Gardner is considered the father of Wicca, but he never actually referred to his religion as Wicca or its followers as Wiccans. Gardner called his religion "The cult of witchcraft" or simply witchcraft. This meant he was using witchcraft as the term for the religion itself (as opposed to a practice within that religion) and if you were a practitioner of the religion, you would be called a witch. Gardner used the term "Wica", with only one "c" to describe witches in plural. So a single witch was a witch but multiple witches were Wica, not "witches."

"Wicca" with two "c's" is the old English word for "witch" and was adopted in the 60's and 70's by the neo-pagan witchcraft community in order to avoid stigma and negative connotation. Just as we face negative connotation with the words witch and witchcraft today, the same stigma was present back then and the neo-pagan witchcraft community was tired of being associated with evil and Satanism.

The use of the terms Wicca, instead of witchcraft and Wiccan instead of witch started to take off around this time and was fueled by Anton Lavey's widely popular book **The Satanic Witch.** Lavey simply stole this historical word that had already been attributed to a totally different set of beliefs and associated it with Satanism. It makes perfect sense that practitioners of witchcraft did not want to be associated with Satanism and therefore adopted the name Wiccan.

Knowing all of this history, some Wiccans who practice and believe most of the Gardnerian practices refuse to call themselves Wiccans. They much rather call themselves witches or "wica" and they say that witchcraft is their religion because that's how Gardner intended it to be. I personally call myself both a witch and a Wiccan because I am a believer in the Wiccan faith and also practice witchcraft. When I go into detail about coming out as a witch, you'll see the importance of using the term Wiccan in order to avoid stigma.

What makes someone a witch?

There is absolutely no one on this earth that can know if you're a witch other than you. As I mentioned above, witchcraft includes so many different practices and beliefs and if you resonate with **any of them**, then you can call yourself a witch. That being said, I know that it can be really hard to pinpoint if you're actually a witch or just enjoy the culture. As I said, many people don't consider themselves witches, simply Wiccans and you might not know if this is your path or if you are in fact a witch. I am going to outline below the characteristics of a witch as well as the signs that you might be one. You can also look into your past or childhood (I have done this) and you'll probably find an instance or two where you were in touch with your witchy side.

Characteristics of a witch

Witches are very in tune with mother nature. They love being outdoors and are able to feel a spiritual energy when in the presence of nature. They also feel an overwhelmingly spiritual connection to the moon and might even feel themselves being drawn to it on the night of the full moon. Witches love animals and plants which often means they are vegetarian or vegan. Witches who do eat meat or processed foods will often feel sluggish or like their energy is being drained. This is especially true after eating fast food.

Witches are very aware of the energy in a location or with a person. They can feel negative or positive energy very strongly. Witches will often feel an overwhelming sense of energy (either good or bad) when in the presence of a location with long histories, such as an ancient ruin, or an old house. They also feel a very strong energy when in the presence of a cemetery, war zone or another place that has a history of death.

Because witches are so in tune with energy, it means they are very empathetic and even emotional. Witches can strongly feel the energy of a person who is suffering. Hospitals are a very overwhelming experience for a witch. He or she will pick up on the energy of the people in the hospital and could even break out into tears for no reason. Witches can be seen as irrationally emotional. This is simply because they can pick up on the energy of other people and so they might cry or get upset even if they have no reason to feel that way. This makes witches feel a strong need to help and heal others which is a big reason for why they partake in witchcraft. Most of the time it is for the healing and wellbeing of those around them.

Witches are human and they look like everyone else to the naked eye but deep down they know they were put on this earth to do more than the average person. For this reason, witches may always carry a sense of feeling different or like they're not like everyone else. This is often very prominent in the childhood and teenage years. They have interests that differ from their schoolmates and often search for movies, books, music and hobbies that are considered alternative.

If a witch is going through teenage years or early adulthood without knowing he/she is a witch, this will cause a lot of frustration and anger. Teen witches who do not know they are witches will have a lot of teen angst whether they show it outwardly or keep it to themselves. This frustration and inner struggle will subside once the witch starts practicing witchcraft.

My experience becoming a witch

Just like teen witches, witches who have been brought up in a religious faith that doesn't allow them to practice witchcraft will also feel an overwhelming sense of frustration. When the witch is presented with the practice of witchcraft, they will start to feel "at home" and like everything makes sense.

This is exactly what I experienced when I was a teenager and was first discovering Wicca and witchcraft. Suddenly, like a ton of bricks, I was hit with the reasons why my life was always filled with such existential crises. My attachment to nature, my attraction to the occult, my ability to sense spirits and the feeling of a feminine goddess all made sense. Wicca was my home, and Christianity, for so many years, had held me back from it.

Now that I have been Wiccan for fifteen years, I often forget that overwhelming feeling of discovery. Although it was an amazing feeling that felt like home, I was absolutely **terrified.** When I would read up on Wiccan culture and beliefs, I felt an overwhelming amount of guilt, like God was watching down on me and knew that I was a trader and a sinner. How could something feel so wrong and so right at the same time? I could feel my mind being opened to a new world that I wanted to explore, but everything about my childhood upbringing was telling me not to go there.

The good news was, I knew I **had to go there** and so I followed that path until eventually, the guilt subsided. I knew this was for me. It's comforting to know that even the deepest traditions that have been ingrained in your soul since childhood cannot keep you from discovering **yourself.**

Once the guilt was gone, I was able to fully enjoy the feeling of relief that Wicca and witchcraft were bringing me. Although this felt freeing and like I had finally found my true identity, I was not ready to come out and tell anyone of my discovery. In fact, I would remain Wiccan in secret for many years.

Signs that you are a witch

If my story resonates with you, you might be a witch. In order to define it once and for all, here are some of the most common signs that you are a witch.

- You feel an overwhelming tie to nature, this includes animals, the environment, plants and the universe.
- You feel the presence of a feminine goddess, especially in the presence of the moon.
- You have premonitions or dreams that come true.
- A deep curiosity or interest in all things occult and magick.
- You have the ability to manifest your desires or have an impact on the universe. For example, if you are thinking about a friend and then they text you. Or you forgot your wallet and a friend offers to pay for dinner without you asking.
- You feel a duty to help and heal others. You want to take away suffering from both humans and animals.
- You don't like the doctor and find yourself rejecting traditional medicine. You even avoid taking things like Advil or cough medicine and would rather use teas, or other natural remedies to heal yourself.
- You're aware of the seasons and know instinctively when the change of season is happening. You can smell the change in the air and feel a difference in temperature much sooner than anyone else.
- You feel crystal energies and are drawn to crystals. You like the way they look and the way they feel.

- You see signs. You pick up on symbols or signs and can interpret the message they are trying to convey. This could be seeing cloud formations, symbols or certain numbers.
- Seeing ghosts or spirits. This can mean physically seeing them or simply feeling their presence.
- You are interested in alternative lifestyles; you don't like things that are considered normal.

There are many more signs that you are a witch but these are the most common ones. You don't need to feel all of these but if you really are a witch, you will likely experience at least a few of the different signs. Remember that the only person who can tell if you're a witch is you!

What Witchcraft is not

There are some misconceptions about witch craft as there is with many things in different religions. These things are misunderstood mainly because people simply do not know anything about the religion or they have been taught that for so long that it is engrained in their brain.

However, witch craft is not all that everyone believes it to be. Here are some of the more common misconceptions about witch craft.

1. Witch craft gives you "ultimate power." This comes from Hollywood and the way that they portray witch craft in the movies that have witch craft in

them. While magic is real and can be used by people, it will not give you the ability to actually do things such as:

Call up cyclones on demand

Turn people into toads

Or any other childhood fantasy that we have had.

This happens when people only take what they know about the Wiccan religion from watching movies. Actually, practicing the religion is ten times different than what you see on the television.

Sorry to say, you are not going to be lighting anyone on fire with your mind anytime soon.

Magic is more of a spiritual awareness in which you can work miracles by using your own energy. You are placing your energy out there into the universe to accomplish something.

2. Wicca and Christianity are utterly opposed: this belief mainly comes from the ancient prejudices that we see in the Old Testament due to people not actually understanding or being able to accept those that are different than them. Those who actually follow the teachings of the Christian god Jesus do not have a problem with anyone who follows another religion.

When you look at the Wiccan religion, there are a few similarities when it comes to the Wiccan religion and the Christian one. Just like with every religion, there are pieces of every religion in another because each religion is slightly based on the other by taking pieces that they like and evolving it to meet what they want to believe in.

3. Witch Craft is Satanism: this is probably one of the biggest misconceptions of witch craft. When you look at it, Satan is not actually a Wiccan deity! The devil is a Christian construct that was used to reflect the fears of those in ancient times about those who practiced other religions. In fact, Wiccan's do not recognize Satan as a real at all. However, there are actual people who worship Satan and they are known as Satanists.

4. Witch Craft is Black magic: black magic is known as magic that is used to hurt someone or something. However, those in the Wiccan religion generally live by the rule of threefold and do not do harm to others. There are those that do practice a negative magic in the Wiccan religion, but they are very few and far between.

5. Witch Craft involves Demon Possession: the belief in demons is up to the individual. However, those in the Wiccan religion generally do not consort with demons or any negative energies for that

matter. Is it possible that some Wiccans actually do deal with demons? Yes. But, it is not part of the actual craft.

Science and Magic

Is there a tie between science and magic? Yes, there very possibly is. But it is not something that anyone can actually tell because the belief in magic all depends on the individual not to mention how you see magic.

However, you have to consider some of the things that we have been able to accomplish as a human race. Would we be able to do this without magic? This would be things such as flying, going to outer space, communicating over long distances, fighting diseases and many more.

So, is there a tie between the two? Who knows, ultimately it is up to you to decide if there is or not. No one can actually disprove the existence of magic because to each person magic is something different.

Ritual and Spell work

Rituals and spell work are actually two very different things. Many people believe that they are the same thing because you can do spell work during a ritual, but it is however very different. Here are some of the differences between the two:

Spell work is a specific formula that you are going to use to shape your circumstances or in order to get a specific outcome.

This usually takes you between space and time and is an act of creation.

Spells are used to instruct, craft, weave, mould, and swirl the different synchronicities.

Spells are usually used to create something while embedding it to a life force within the living matrix.

And spells add more energy to the energy web that surrounds us all.

Rituals are the fostering of a connection between your mind body and soul.

They can be either simple or complex, but are usually meant to touch something deep within your core.

Rituals are prayers that are set in motion to make a physical gesture that merges within or even without but it is always something that integrates with your presence.

And rituals are held in a space that helps you to maintain an internal state until it becomes a default space for you.

Ultimately, rituals are going to give you a structure that provides you with a safe space in which you can open up to your innermost self, and these are used for honoring. Spells however are going to be able to transform you in essence so that you go from one state of consciousness and move to another. These are given through a form of energy.

Tools of Witchcraft

There are always going to be tools that you need in order to complete anything, and just like anything else, witch craft requires certain tools in order to make it work properly. Below are some of the tools you'll need when practicing witch craft.

1. The witch: Very obviously you're going to need yourself.
2. The athame: this is a knife that is often related to the male genitalia
3. The broom: this is used for cleaning out the ritual areas so that you can start fresh. It is also used in rituals such as jumping the broom during a hand fasting ceremony or as a sign of protection to keep away negative energies.
4. The bell: this is used to open and close your circle, or even to ward off negative energies while inviting positive energies.
5. The Cauldron: very obviously this is going to be where you are going to mix together your ingredients for your spells and is often used to represent the concept of reincarnation.
6. The chalice: this is a cup that is used to represent the female genitalia
7. The clothing Magickal: this consists of robes, caps, and any other jewelry you may use if you do not participate in skyclad

8. The paton or altar pentacle: this is usually something that is inscribed with the five-pointed star in a circle.

9. The staff: this is used to hold banners as well as represent some elements.

10. The sword: this is used much like the athame but however is more for outdoor rituals.

11. The incense burner: incense is used as representing the elements of air and fire at once. Both of the elements can be used for purification.

12. The wand: this is not something that you have to have, but the wand represents the element of air and can be used to cast your circle or to direct your energy in a magical way.

How to Become a Wiccan or a Witch

This is not something that you're going to wake up and just decide that you're going to do one day. You are also not born with it. More often than not, it is something that you're going to just accidentally come across one day unless you happen to have grown up with it being practiced around you.

The only way that you can actually become a Wiccan or witch is to do your research and decide if it is even the religion that is for you in the first place. Make sure that you understand the beliefs of the different practices and that you believe in what the Wiccan faith is actually about.

Ultimately the choice is yours to decide if you want to follow the Wiccan religion or not. Listen to your inner voice and if you believe that this is the right path for you. Do not let anyone pressure you into doing it because if you do then you may come to regret your decision. Not only that, but the ritual of becoming a Wiccan or witch is something that needs to be yours and yours alone.

It is important for you to design your ritual the way that you want it because you are dedicating yourself to the craft, you're going to want to make your dedication ritual one that you never regret.

Chapter 3 Intermediate Wicca

After you have begun learning more about the basics of Wicca, you can start understanding some of the other principals and beliefs.

Enlightenment and Magic

Enlightenment means to illuminate, to be able to see the truth, to give light to, to give clarification etc. For Wiccans, to become enlightened means to understand life, and is also known as awakening. It is the process of us understanding our role in the universe, and we can only achieve this through our unique personal experiences, it cannot be taught.

Enlightenment is a continual course and not a final goal to be reached. It can come in little drops, like the first drops of rain, or it can be a sudden downpour. By being aware, even slightly, we continue to be enlightened about something. If we claim that we know everything, then we have strayed from the path of enlightenment.

Our hunger for truth and wisdom will vary from individual to individual and depends on different factors. Sometimes life, and its many stresses, can cause you to focus on just getting through the day. For those who have the opportunity to contemplate and mediate on deep questions, such questions asked include, what am I doing here? Who are the gods? Who am I? What's the meaning of life?

These questions cannot be answered by anyone but you. If you want to understand them, however, you must work to understand them. You cannot find the answers to these questions just by thinking and analytic process. You can, however, ask these questions to other people and discuss them, helping you to deepen your knowledge.

The Oath of Secrecy

All Wiccans who are initiated into a coven, or group, are asked to swear the oath of secrecy. Most of us don't have to live with these kinds of oaths on a daily basis unless we are in the military, the medical field, or the police force; we live in democratic societies and censorship is considered a negative thing.

There are many reasons why Wiccans have oaths of secrecy. First, the Burning Times were a period of persecution and death for Wiccans, Witches, and Pagans. Many countries, including America and several European countries, still experience the 'religious right', where strong Christian believers have caused Wiccans to lose custody of their children, their homes, their jobs, their friends, and sometimes even their own lives, due to being Wiccan. Depending on where you live, you may not have many difficulties, but there will be some for others. As such, you should never 'out' another Wiccan unless they give you permission. You never know what difficulties they may face in their lives.

Intermediate Level Spells

A Love Spell to Attract the Attention of the One You Desire
You will need:

- An orange candle
- Marjoram essential oil
- Dish
- A picture/photo of the one you desire

Cast your circle as usual and place the photo or picture of the one you desire in the dish before you. Take the marjoram essential oil and anoint the candle with it. Place the candle in the dish and light it. Repeat the following as you stare into the flames:

By the light of this candle

I turn your eyes

I turn your eyes,

I turn your head

By my thighs

By my thighs,

Through marjoram I seek

I find you

I find you,

Through flame and desire

It becomes truth

It becomes truth.

Now let the candle burn down to the base without moving the photo. If you wish, you can sprinkle some of the melted wax on the route to your house from your desired one's home.

A Spell to Break a Love Spell

While we may have good intentions when it comes to love spells, there are times when we make mistakes. In those instances, it is imperative that you release that person from the spell. The following spell is a way of releasing that person.

You will need the following:

- A black/white candle
- A black cloth
- Myrrh essential oil
- A pin

A white candle can be substituted for a black candle if you don't have one available. Take the pin and carve the name of the person you wish to free on the side of the candle with it. Take the myrrh essential oil and anoint the candle with it.

Light the candle and meditate. Visualize the spell breaking as you stare into the flames. Repeat the following three times:

As this candle burns, you are now free

The bindings no longer hold thee

So, mote it be.

Allow the candle to burn down completely. When cool, take the wax and wrap it into the cloth. Throw it into a water source (such as a river, a stream, a pond, the ocean etc.) but not a wishing well. Burying it in the ground is an alternative if there are no water sources available to you. The person under the love spell is now free.

A Spell for More Confidence

There are times when we could all do with a little confidence boost. This spell can help encourage you using self-affirmations and sounds. Centuries ago, bells were used to drive off evil spirits and demons, but today we can use them to banish the demons and negativity within us.

You will need:

A bell

Music

Cast your circle on the night of a full moon. This is a time of new beginnings. Decide on a self-affirmation you want to use prior to entering your circle. Play the music you wish and allow your energy to rise up as it plays. When you feel your energy is at its highest point, take your bell and dance with the music. Scream or cry out to the world your affirmation nine times.

Chapter 4 Advanced Wicca

Now you have a further understanding on basic and intermediate Wicca and have casted several different types of spells, it is time to learn more advance topics and spells.

Pendulums

Pendulums have been a popular feature in Magick for centuries. Even in ancient times, pendulums had been used in order to gain knowledge. Today, many people try to determine the gender of a baby still in the womb using a pendulum. They are an easy way for Wiccans to use.

There is a stigma towards magickal tools for non-Wiccans. Despite their misgivings, there is nothing evil or any entities within pendulums or any other tool. These tools are an extension of the information that is within you. The information that you receive and use is what you have gained through listening and being aware of the universe on a subconscious level.

The easiest way to use a pendulum is to hold the top of the string or chain between your thumb and forefinger. Keep the area clear of things so nothing gets in its way. Now think of the question you want to ask and the direction it swings gives you your answer – these questions are usually in the form of yes or no answers. Maps can also be positioned underneath the pendulum to receive answers to more detailed questions.

The direction of the pendulum swings in, to give you your yes or no answer, depends on the user. You can program it, as such, so you can find out what direction means yes, and what direction means no. Ask several questions, such as **is my name Lisa? Am I a girl?** Etc. You will discover for yourself what direction means yes or no.

Advanced Wiccan Spells

A Spell to Bring Back a Lost Love

If you are searching for a way to bring back a lost love and get another chance, this spell is ideal for you. It doesn't necessarily mean that they will fall in love with you, as that would be a violation of the Wiccan code of freedom, but instead it is a way of two previous lovers crossing paths again which in turn, could give you both the opportunity to rekindle the flame.

You will need the following:

- A quiet space to work in
- A white candle
- A black candle
- A small white candle
- A white ribbon
- A black ribbon

- A brown candle

Please note, black candles are not considered evil – they are a representation of the feminine, much like yin and yang in Chinese philosophy. If you are a woman seeking to meet a man then you would use the black candle to represent yourself; if you are a man seeking a woman, then you would use the white candle to represent yourself; if you seeking to meet someone of the same sex, then the black candle represents the more submissive/passive person.

Nine days before the new moon, find a quiet spot to work in. Dress the black candle first, thinking of the more submissive person during that time. Next, dress the white candle, whilst thinking of the more masculine person during that time. Finally, dress the brown candle. The brown candle is the representation of your reunion, so keep it in mind as you dress it.

Next, take a few moments to mediate. Keep thinking of the reunion you are hoping for before lighting the candle, which is a representation of you with the small white candle. Say:

I am drawn to you, let you be drawn to me

As I wish, so mote it be.

Repeat it nine times. Keep the reunion in your mind at all times and then blow out the candle. The following night, repeat this process, but move the white candle closer to the black one a little. For the next six nights, do the same, but move the candle closer each time. On the ninth night, do the same as previous nights, but after repeating the spell nine times, use both candles to burn the brown candle. Let the brown candle burn down and then take the wax from the black, white, and brown candles and bury them within the ground.

A Full Moon Money Spell

The Full Moon Money Spell should be cast on a full moon as this period is when magick is at its greatest strength and result in positive outcomes. This is a great spell for when you are experiencing a tight budget or if you have a monetary emergency.

You will need the following:

- A Cauldron
- Water
- Silver coins
- A white candle
- A green candle

On the night of the full moon, cast your circle and place the cauldron with fresh clean water in it in the center. Position it so it is directly underneath the moonlight. Light the candles and drop silver coins into it. Hover your hand over the water as though you are scooping out money. Repeat the following spell:

Lady of the Moon, grant your blessing soon

Fill my hands with silver, come hither with gold

All you can give, I can hold.

Repeat the spell three times and leave the water in the cauldron underneath the moonlight for that night. In the morning, pour the water into the ground, but not the coins. You should be blessed soon.

A Wishing Spell

If you are looking for a way to make the impossible come true, then this wishing spell is just what you need.

You will need the following:

- A white candle
- Water

This spell should be cast on the night of a full moon. Cast your circle and step inside. Light the white candle and focus on the divine (this could be a manifestation/aspect of the divine, such as a particular god or goddess like Hecate, Artemis, Epona etc.). Position the water on your altar. Release all negative energies in your thoughts and desires and concentrate on the good, positive things. When you feel all the negativity slide away, pick up the water and thank the divine (or Goddess if you will) for altering your thoughts and then drink the water. Close the circle.

A wish spell initially seems simple, but it is more for advance spell casters as it means you have freed yourself, or cleansed yourself, of all negative thoughts. The wish may or may not come true, but it is an energy manipulation and won't work on casters who don't continue to work on their spiritual side.

Chapter 5 Wicca: Covens, Circles, and Solitary Practice

As you continue to delve deeper into understanding Wicca, you will learn about covens and circles and the difference between them and solitary practice. You will also discover that it is quite tasking to directly access other Wicca practitioners. This is because there is no central place of worship where, as a beginner, you can go to seek insight and guidance.

"Coven" is a Latin word that means to "meet up." It was widely used during the Middle Ages to describe social gatherings of different types. In the early 1600s, covens were more associated with witches. Covens gained further popularity in the mid-20th century as the "Old Religion" was being re-introduced.

A coven was initially a 13-member of witches who secretly met to practice. A coven was comprised of a High Priest and a High Priestess who spoke to the God and the Goddess. Today, however, covens do not necessarily have to have 13 members. Different Wiccans were initiated into the tradition following either the belief systems of Alex Sanders or Gerald Gardner. Some Wiccan covens will follow the initial traditions while others embrace different varied beliefs.

Most Wiccan covens have a set-out tradition of initiating new members into the coven. These set-out traditions are custom and the coven requires the new members to fully invest themselves in the initiation. Once the new member is initiated, other requirements follow to ascertain the new member's commitment to the coven. There are different levels of initiation and the new members follow certain custom conditions to get from the first to the third degree. The prerequisites to progress from one degree to another are dependent on the coven a member is following.

As a common practice, a Wiccan coven will mark the Sabbats and Esbats celebrations. Others will also mark other days between these two celebrations. For these celebrations, if a coven intends to include a new member, then they will invest their time and energy into getting the individual ready. Members of the same coven are family to one another. The members have a very close bond. Therefore, when a coven intends to welcome a new individual, all the members are invested in the process including the individual in question.

If you are a beginner in Wicca, it is highly unlikely that you will immediately join a coven. This is because most covens require one to have been practicing for more than a year especially before you can go through the initiation process. This is a great requirement because it ensures that the individual is fully certain and committed to being part of a Wiccan coven. Understandably so, if joining a coven is difficult for you, you might consider finding other practicing Wiccans within your locale and joining their circle or you could simply start your own circle.

A circle is a gathering of individuals who are Wiccan practitioners. They meet to talk and explore the Craft. It could conceivably include a normal Sabbat and additionally Esbat celebration. However, on the off chance that these occasions are marked, participation is common but not compulsory.

Contingent upon the general inclinations of the gathering, there might be numerous individuals, some of whom drop in and out as it suits them, or only a couple of consistently included companions. The structure of a circle is commonly free and doesn't require official inception or include a setup chain of importance. Amateurs are regularly welcome, and you're probably going to locate a wide scope of information and experience levels around, where everybody contributes their very own point of view.

If you can't locate any similarly invested people in your general vicinity, don't be concerned. There are numerous online networks of Wiccans and different Witches to study, and there are likewise numerous advantages to solo practice. Actually, by far most of the Wiccans in the 21st century are solo practitioners. Becoming more acquainted with the otherworldly and mystical parts of the Universe all alone can be extremely fulfilling!

In case you're sure you need to work with others, be that as it may, you can approach the Goddess and God to attract the opportune individuals to you. At that point be tolerant, trust divine planning, and your coven or circle will, in the end, show up in your life.

As a solo practitioner, we can explore how you can initiate and dedicate yourself to the practice. A custom of self-commitment may look like parts of a coven initiation to changing degrees, but since single Witches can structure and play out this custom in any capacity they like, it is on a very basic level diverse experience.

Self-dedication happens entirely without having to conform to anyone else terms. The dedication you're announcing in such a custom is true to your internal identity, or to any gods you may join into your training, and to the heavenliness of the Universe as you comprehend it. It is anything but a promise to some other individual, or passage into a gathering of individual experts. What's more, since this experience is entirely among you and the universe, you can consider it whatever you like—initiation, self-commitment, self-initiation, or something different completely, if that is the thing that sounds good to you.

In spite of the fact that this is an altogether different ordeal from that of a coven initiation, there are still critical parallels on the adventure to this achievement nonetheless. In the first place, obviously, is crafted by truly figuring out the Craft—investigating conceivable roads as far as learning customs, getting a sense of what impacts you and what doesn't, and proceeding to seek information to any extent you feel applicable and as broadly as possible. It's generally prescribed to go through a year and multi-day contemplating the Craft before attempted your self-initiation, yet you can positively take longer on the off chance that you understand the process.

When you feel prepared to step toward initiation, you can begin contemplating what this will mean to you.

In case you find yourself interested, you can take parts of one practice and other parts from another, making up your own way toward Wicca practice. Yet, you can at present concentrate on learning as you work your way toward the point where you feel prepared for initiation. You can "allocate" yourself a specific measure of study every week and arrange your investigations around explicit themes. For example, the Triple Goddess or the Wheel of the Year, and additionally peruse every one of the books composed by a specific writer before proceeding onward to another one. On the other hand, you might find that you are interested in a diversity of books, following your intuition so that you are able to grasp from these books the information you feel is relevant to you.

With regards to the Wiccan initiation custom itself, you can structure your own process of initiation. Simply realize that the subtleties are less critical than your genuine want to formalize your pledge to the Wiccan lifestyle. You can even ask the Goddess and God to enable you to pick your best method.

Self-dedication is an individual choice that nobody can make for you, except if you are looking for enrollment in a coven. It's really a completely discretionary thing. In any case, regardless of where you look for initiation, realize that a solitary custom won't abruptly launch you into an out and out mystical presence, or certification that you'll remain on this specific route for eternity. There are Witches who have worked for their entire lives without experiencing initiation, and a lot of beginners who lost enthusiasm for Wicca did not follow through. For a long time during the initial phases, it will be dependent upon you to keep choosing your way, in your own particular manner and at your very own pace.

Wicca is regularly thought of as an approximately organized or even totally unstructured custom which is quite deep and for some individuals who were brought up in progressively formal composed religions, this is certainly part of the charm. In any case, there is a central component of Wicca that serves to unite individuals around an aggregate center, which is made up of Wiccan customs.

Regardless of whether the event is a Sabbat, an Esbat or an achievement, for example, a handfasting (wedding), an inception, or an end of-life service, covens and circle individuals will accumulate to share their love and respect of the Goddess and God, and commend the initiation to be found in the continuous cycles of life. While most Wiccan ceremonies are held in private, a few covens will once in a while hold theirs out in the open, with the goal that all who wish to watch can come and get familiar with the Craft. Numerous Wiccan circles do likewise, and may even welcome general society to take an interest.

Obviously, solo ceremonies are no less noteworthy, and singular Wiccans realize that as they venerate at each point along the Wheel of the Year, they are including their own light and capacity to the group otherworldly energy on these exceptional events.

Beautiful and mysterious, Wiccan ceremonies can take various structure, with no two occasions being actually similar. Some might be very organized and elaborate. This is frequently the situation with coven ceremonies. However, since most covens keep the subtleties of their customs secret - known only by initiated individuals - it's hard to portray them with much precision. Different ceremonies, especially those by single and varied Wiccans, might be genuinely basic by comparison, and may even be made up on the spur of the moment.

The substance of some random Wiccan custom will rely upon the event. For instance, Esbats, or Full Moon festivities, are centered exclusively upon the Goddess, while Sabbats respect the co-inventive connection between the Goddess and the God. In spite of all the conceivable varieties, nonetheless, there are a couple of essential components that will, in general, be incorporated into what we may call an "ordinary" custom.

To start with, there is decontamination, both of the celebrant(s) and where the custom is held. This can occur as a custom shower, as well as a smirching service to expel any undesirable energies from the custom space, regardless of whether it's an outside region or inside the home. Smearing includes the consuming of consecrated herbs, for example, sage, rosemary or lavender.

Setting up the altar happens first. A few Wiccans can keep a raised area permanently set up in their homes. However, even in this situation, it will probably be enriched contrastingly relying upon the event, for example, getting fall foliage for Mabon (the Autumn Equinox) or Samhain (otherwise called Halloween.) The special stepped area is part of the different Wiccan customs and will be decorated in accordance with the event that is being celebrated.

Next comes the casting of the circle, an action that sets a limit between the spiritual realm and the mundane physical world. The altar is normally the focal point of the circle, with a lot of space for all required to work unreservedly inside the circle, with no incidental venturing outside of the boundary, which is thought to contain energy. The circle might be set apart with ocean salt in a long line, a few stones, herbs or candles. There are numerous techniques for circle-casting that you will discover for yourself as you practice.

When the circle is cast, the ritual starts. The invocations here can change, yet ordinarily the God and Goddess are invited to join the ritual and afterward, the four Elements—Earth, Air, Fire, and Water—are summoned (In numerous customs, a fifth Element—Akasha, or Spirit—is additionally brought in.) In different conventions, this invocation, known as calling the Quarters, and the four bearings (North, East, South and West), is tended to, either rather than or notwithstanding the Elements.

When these actions have occurred, the core of the celebration starts. To begin with, the aim of the ceremony is expressed— regardless of whether it's to praise a Sabbat or an Esbat, or maybe to pray to the God and Goddess for the benefit of somebody who needs it or some other sort of help.

After the intention is expressed, the fundamental body of the custom may comprise of different exercises. The point of convergence might be the execution of a custom dramatization. For example, reenacting scenes from antiquated legends or sonnets—or other ritualistic material, contingent upon the convention of Wicca the gathering is following. Single Wiccans may likewise peruse from old enchanted messages, or make their very own verse for the event. Reciting, singing, moving as well as other ceremonial motions might form a part of the ceremony, and the season in which the ceremony is held will have great significance. Supplications may be offered, regardless of whether they are close to home or for the benefit of others. Truth be told, it's regular in a few conventions to use customs to encompass not only thoughts of those within the coven, but also for those outside of it.

In numerous celebrations, a service known as "cakes and brew" (or "cakes and wine") is an imperative part of Wiccan history. Sustenance and drink are offered and emblematically imparted to the God and Goddess, ordinarily toward the end of the ritual.

Chapter 6 Wicca: Book(s) of Shadows

A Book of Shadows is fairly similar to a diary, however with an unequivocally otherworldly and supernatural core interest. It might incorporate spells, names, and dates of Sabbats and Esbats, mantras and other custom dialect, arrangements of enchanted correspondences for hues, precious stones, and herbs, and a large group of another valuable supernatural randomness.

The Book of Shadows is basically a cutting-edge grimoire—a term utilized in the nineteenth century to portray writings covering different Witchcraft activities, for example, enchanted hypothesis, portrayals of ceremonies, guidance in spell work and divination frameworks, magical rationalities, and other exclusive data. Instances of grimoires can be found all through the Middle Ages and much prior, at least going back to stone tablets found in old Egypt and Mesopotamia.

It was Gerald Gardner who received the expression "Book of Shadows" as a title for his very own coven's grimoire, which was intended to be kept a mystery from everyone except the chosen individuals from his coven. The material was added to and updated as time went on, with the understanding that these practices ought not to wind up static and settled, but rather ought to rather stay dynamic, with new ages of Witches including and subtracting from them as they saw fit.

As Witchcraft developed into Wicca, it moved into new and different customs gaining new insight adding to the making of new Book(s) of Shadows – However, not all Wiccans keep a Book(s) of Shadows to record their mystical knowledge and magical experiences. Most covens that abide by the old Wicca traditions keep their mystical knowledge and magical experiences a mystery.

Despite the fact that it is unexpected for a Wiccan to completely share with others their Book of Shadows, it is for that reason that knowledge about it has come into the public domain and gained interest from people. In the current day of the Internet, some Wiccan practitioners actually share their Book of Shadows online. Therefore, the mystery that surrounds Wicca continues to diminish. However, it is important to note that it is quite standard for Wiccans to conceal their Book of Shadows from other people who might not understand the Craft.

Chapter 7 Wicca and Magic

When talking about Wicca, it is almost impossible not to talk about magic. There exists a huge association between the two. Magic as a tradition has existed longer than Wicca actually has. Magic and Wicca as traditions both bear similarities to one another. It is these similarities that give Magic a "Wiccan" feel. Pagan communities and Wiccans in their circles refer to the tradition of Magic as "Magick." Wiccans use magic as a way of tapping into the divine energy flow of nature to seek guidance and insight into their lives as well as for the benefit of other people.

People who are uninformed and ignorant about magic conceive it to be something very different. This ranges from perceiving magicians as illusionists who create anything from an illusion of a rabbit coming out of a hat to an animation of a film character that disappears at the snap of their fingers. However, for people who practice magic, magic is perhaps one of the most incredible traditions of the world.

Magic as an English word that is associated with the French word "Magique" and made a debut in the late 1300s. The meaning of magic in French is the special craft of having an impact on circumstances by the use of secret powers. For the 21st century witch practicing magic, magic is intentionally taking part in the powers of the universe by directing nature's energies to create desired change in one's life. Witches utilize different techniques to take part in the power that is in charge of the occurrences of the Universe. They do so to impact their own realities with the realization that the truth is liquid and is always changing.

"Magick" is spelled so because it sets it apart from other forms of powers that were used by illusionists and other performers who were very common then. This spelling originated from Aleister Crowley a pioneer in the development of British Witchcraft. This was in the late 19th Century leading up to the mid-20th Century - a period that led up to the Wicca tradition.

Magic is also commonly referred to by its practitioners as "Black magic" or the "Craft." As mentioned earlier, magic is the ability of an individual to affect change. Just like the Wiccan tradition, there is no solitary methodology in the practice of magic.

The practice of magic is centered on affecting change in one's personal life. This change could be desired in one's wealth, love or health. A person may practice magic to gain riches, to quickly heal from a physical ailment or to get help in finding love. Another reason to practice magic would be to protect oneself from negative energies.

A number of witches work toward the prosperity of the community over individual gain. A Wiccan circle, for instance, may practice a magic ritual to send positive energies to a person suffering from a physical ailment to heal quickly or to the victims of an earthquake. A number of Wiccans use the Sabbats and Esbats celebrations as a time to practice magic that will allow them to reflect upon their lives and practice. This could be seen in a very similar light to the way in which Christians use prayer for the greater good.

Today, the practice of Witchcraft encompasses different methodologies. Magic involves charms, spells, rituals, celebrations, dancing among others. The practice may include customs from a very long time ago or new and spontaneous customs. Magic practiced by Wiccan is informed by Freemasons and the Hermetic Order of the Golden Dawn. These customs include the use of images and signs that guide energies toward desired outcomes. This is commonly referred to as "high magic." "Low magic" on the other hand is the use of magical rituals that are a few centuries old that belong to old social conventions in Europe.

A great number of Wiccans practice magic using ritual tools such as herbs, crystals and candles among other things. With the realization that the Earth is our home, Witches work with the knowledge of the energies present in nature's process of birth, death, and change. The energies present in these processes of nature are used by the witches in their magical practice. For example, a Wiccan candle magic ritual involves using the flame to consume an unwanted outcome or to enhance an outcome by timing one's desires with the minute the Moon turns to a full Moon. The practice of magic is highly rewarding if you care enough to put in effort and commitment to it.

It is important to note that not all Wiccans practice magic. Wiccans who practice magic are guided by the Wiccan Rede, a rule that will be mentioned several times in this book. The rule requires that no harm is done to other living beings and things in one's practice of magic. Wiccans are keen to ensure that the outcome of their magical ritual does not negatively affect the beneficiary or themselves as it could backfire. Magic should not be practiced to affect another person who has not chosen to be part of it.

In addition, Wiccans also work to ensure that they avoid any coincidental negative effects with the practice of magic as it reveals itself in the physical realm. To achieve this, after a magical spell is cast by a Wiccan, it is concluded by the expression "with damage to none" or any other similar expression that means the same. This speaks to the universe while reminding the witch that only kind and well-meaning impacts are sought by the use of magic.

There exist naturally skilled Witches in the Wiccan circles. If you want to become skilled in magic, then you should be prepared to practice consistently, to be still and to learn from your different experiences. As a beginner, remember that it is very normal to experience no outcomes in your initial practice in magic. Be sure to study as much as you can about magic and work as an individual to avoid negativity, which is often experienced in the early stages of the craft.

To demystify the association between Wicca and magic, it is important to note that magic is not particular to any spiritual or magical path. Notably, there are many magic traditions; some that stem from Latin America which are the healing deeds of curanderos to the practice of Heka, which were the hoodoo charms of the Appalachians in Egypt. These magical practices have been passed down from generation to generation over centuries and are still in practice in some parts of the world. Your magic will be a combination of these customs to which you will add your own.

Wiccan magic is associated with ancient practices that stem from the magical traditions of Hermetic philosophies. Thee Hermetic philosophies were rediscovered during the Renaissance period. In addition, Wiccan magic is also derived from European folk healing. Just like its fluidity, the magical spells as practiced by Wiccan practitioners are constantly changing through the experimentation of energies found in Nature and all of its creation.

There are different types of magic practiced by Wiccans. They range from ritual ecstatic dance, divination, clearing energies, dream pillows and charms. The ritual tools just like the types of initiation can essentially come from anywhere. They could be ribbon scraps, humble stones, wands that are encrusted in jewels and cauldrons that are cast in iron.

Wiccan magic is a personal artistic style and practitioners are free to explore their preferences and styles. However, there are some norms of Wiccan magic that are embraced by both seasoned and beginning Witches.

Candle magic

This is used and recommended to beginners. Candle magic can be explored using basic candle spells that will enable the beginner to build on their capabilities. The intention is stated and the flame is used as a medium. The burning of the candle, hence its disappearance, symbolizes the departure from the material to an ethereal plan carrying with it the magical request also referred to as the intention. This transformation that is witnessed with the physical eye enables a beginner to associate the visualization of the manifestation process.

Crystal magic

Although crystals have been determined as inorganic, they are believed to be alive in carrying energy. Crystals have the power to bequeath energy to organic things such as plants, animals and human beings. They are nature's intensely beautiful and mystical creations. It is a great way to become acquainted with the universe. The power that is inherent in other natural elements such a rivers or wind is also present in crystals and other mineral stones. Intentions as energy can be sent out to the universe using the chosen crystals as a conduit of energy.

Herbal magic

This type is very practical and can be practiced with herbs and plants that are already in the kitchen - hence the practicality. Herbs are very diverse and one can easily create their own magical crafts. It requires patience, which makes it a rewarding Craft for a Witch. Herbal magic is very hands on and one can create dream pillows, spells jars among other charms. People have been known to create incense and oils from herbs making their work even more magical.

Although crystals, herbs and candles are commonly used in magic, there are other magical staples used that you can explore as you grow in your practice.

Chapter 8 Aspects of the God – the Oak and Holly King, and the Horned God

Just as with the Triple Goddess mirroring the changing of the seasons both in the natural world and in our human existence, so does the pagan God reflect the wax and wane of life and the ebb and flow of death and rebirth.

The Wheel of the Year is something that will be covered in depth later on in this book, but a brief explanation is necessary to understand the God's role in the seasons. Pagan holidays are such: the year culminates and starts anew with Samhain (pronounced as **sowhen**), around the time of modern Halloween and after the harvest season is fully finished. Next is Yule—which marks the winter solstice. After Yule, we have Imbolc in early February, then Ostara in March at the spring equinox, Beltane on the first of May, and finally Litha, which marks the highest point of summer and the summer solstice. Lammas follows Litha in August when the crops are ready and ripe, and finally, Mabon is when the harvest is collected for the last time.

The Oak King rules over one half of the year; **the Holly King** the other. The Oak King is born at Yuletide when the world is at its darkest; this aspect of the god brings us to hope that the Sun will return and harvest will bring food once again. As he grows, becoming fully mature at Beltane, he in hand with the goddess awakens the Earth and the plants lying dormant beneath the frost of winter. The Oak King is at his strongest at the summer solstice, just as the wheat and the corn crops are at their tallest just before they are harvested. At Lammas, the Oak King's strength begins to wane, and it is the Holly King—born during the summer solstice—who moves from infant to boyhood, to fully stand in the place he has inherited from the Oak King at Yule.

Other legends depict the Oak and Holly kings in timeless, eternal battle, each defeating the other, year after year. Sir Gawain and the Green Knight, it is believed, was inspired by the folklore of the two godly kings.

The Horned God

The Horned God has often been falsely accused of having a correlation with Satan, but again, Wiccans do not hold such beliefs. The Horned God is a nature god, a protector of all things wild that live in the woods, plains, streams, lakes, and oceans. Images depicting the Horned God have been created by humans as long ago as the Paleolithic era of our world. The Horned God brings life to the Earth's rich womb, ensuring that the world's creatures will have food during every season. There are many manifestations of the Horned God throughout the world's cultures and peoples.

A list of horned gods:

Cernunnos. This European god is one of the oldest known horned gods and was worshipped widely across Western Europe. Today he is best known in pagan depictions of "the Wild Hunt" where supernatural beings chase stags across a wild landscape, and as the iconic "Green Man", which has even shown up on bottles of craft-brewed beer in the Eastern US in a brewery of the same name.

Another name for Cernunnos is **Herne**, a British god and also depicted in scenes of the Wild Hunt.

A frightening depiction of Cernunnos can be found in Shakespeare's **The Merry Wives of Windsor**. While Cernunnos is a benevolent god, he is foremost a god of wild creatures, and cannot be tamed. He is everything wild and free on the Earth: the wind rustling unhindered through the waving currents of grass, the thunder of hoof beats of the buffalo herd, the lonely cry of the eagle as it coasts past craggy, mountain peaks. We may pray to him to rouse our inner wildness and give thanks for our place on this glorious planet called Earth.

When praying to Cernunnos as **Herne**, it is said to be quite effective to find a peaceful place to sit in the forest and tell Herne all of your troubles. In this aspect, the Horned God is fatherly and listens to his children with patience and compassion.

Cernunnos' favored colors are green and brown.

Dionysus (also known as Bacchus). This Greek god rules over the chaotic domains of intoxication, untethered masculine sexuality, hallucinations, and dreams. He is said to have a dual personality and is thought to have the ability to heal mental illness and disorders. He presides over the shaman as they walk through the spirit world, as well as the dreamer as they march across the dreamscape. Partaking in wine means sharing blessings with Dionysus. Prayers to him should be thoughtful and careful, although a simple prayer of thanks before meditation or sleep, or going out on the town to barhop, would be just enough.

Dionysus' favored colors are deep red and purple.

Osiris. This Egyptian god was often depicted with the horns of a bull and is a fertility god. Throughout the legends that surround him, Osiris was reincarnated several times, and often as a heavenly bull. Osiris rules rebirth, reincarnation, and the underworld, and delivers merciful judgment to the dead as they enter his world. He is described as "the Lord of love" as well as "the Lord of Silence." Pray to Osiris when you need clarity and strength to navigate life's more difficult moments. You may not hear his words, but you will feel them in your heart.

Osiris' favored colors are green and gold.

Pan. This Greek god invites us to put aside our worries, for a while, and enjoy life. Pan rules the natural world, but with a lighthearted hand; he invites us to put aside our ego and get our hands dirty in the mud of life, to feel the soil beneath our feet and the Sun on our heads. Pray to Pan when you feel overburdened by life's stresses, and he will show you the way to more carefree days.

Curiously, the word **panic** derives from the same origin as this horned god's name. Pan's bellowing cry has the power to incite panic in his enemy, but he does not do this out of malice or boredom. Legends tell of him inciting panic and chaos in warring armies, but he never chose a side to win over the other; Pan simply dislikes war. He prefers to enjoy his life and hopes you do too.

Pan's favored colors are brown and green.

The Elements

When we talk about "the elements" in this section, we are discussing not the elements of the periodic table, but the more ancient knowledge concerning the elements used in rituals in Wicca and other pagan faiths. The most common are the four elements, but actually, there are five, and they correspond to the points of the right-side up pentagram, beginning at the top: Spirit, Water, Fire, Earth, and Air. For the purposes of introduction, however, we are going to focus on the primary four. If you were to stand in the middle of a compass rose, facing north, you would be addressing the Earth element. If you were to turn clockwise—which we call "sunwise" in Wicca—and stop at the East, you would be addressing the element of Air. One more sunwise stop on the compass rose and you arrive at the South, and the element of Fire, and the last stop—the West—has you facing the element of Water.

Earth

The element of Earth represents our home, and everything it takes to create that home: it is the planet, the bedrock, and magma that shapes it, the mountains that rise from its stony face, and the sand that glitters at the edges of the seas.

Earth is where we begin, and where we end (until we rise into Spirit). Before any ritual, Wiccans "cast a circle", which means they inscribe an invisible, protective barrier around their sacred space—insulating them from the outside world and the unseen that might draw close in curiosity to their magical work. When casting a circle, each of the four elements is addressed, and faced—and Earth is always first.

Earth represents foundations, the material with which to build, and raw material (as well as potential). It is logic, research, ancestry, and family. Earth adores the student and the scholar but also favors the farmer and the hunter. The suit of pentacles of the tarot is connected to the element of Earth.

Ideas connected with Earth:

Abundance

Wealth

Prosperity

Wisdom

Knowledge

Growth (and decay)

Harvest and planting (reaping and sowing)

Inheritance

Ancestors

In the magical world, certain creatures and beings are associated with the Earth element, such as gnomes, brownies, trolls, and giants (particularly from Norse legend). Mark an area on your property with a collection of stones or crystals to let the Earth elementals know you have provided a safe space for them when they stop by.

On your altar: To represent the element of Earth on your altar, a dish of kosher or pink salt, a favorite rock, and a potted plant all work well.

Air

The element of Air brings us the swiftness of communication and ideas. The god Mercury is a perfect example of a god of air—he connects us all with a network of information and constant contact. The element of Air represents new beginnings and renewal, just as the winds can carry seeds across the ocean from one continent to the next, so can the Air element incite sweeping change over the world.

Birds are natural messengers of the Air element, and their visits and sightings should be taken into consideration when you want change, news, or encouragement.

The element of Air is connected with the suit of swords of the tarot.

Ideas connected with Air:

Movement

Divination

Scholarly pursuits

Courage

Communication

Song

Prayer

Destruction (think tornados and storms)

Change

Some magical creatures associated with Air are sylphs, bennu, chi spirits (Chinese house spirits akin to brownies), gryffins, and rocks. Light an offering of incense to the air creatures at dawn or sunset.

On your altar: To represent the element of Air on your altar, a feather or feathered fan, a stick of incense, or an origami crane are all suitable.

Fire

The element of Fire represents passion and vitality. We are drawn to fire, and yet if we touch it, we might be harmed. Too much passion also often incites chaos. A backyard bonfire unchecked might burn down a house.

Still, there is nothing most Wiccan celebrants enjoy more than to gather around a roaring fire with their community. Something about the dancing flames is both soothing and inspiring.

Fire brings us both inspiration, and innovation—with it we can chemically alter things, make things rise, and make things fly. Fire warms us in the coldest heart of winter, and fire is even necessary for some trees to spread their seed. One of the most simple and powerful means of meditation is to light a single candle and watch its flame as you breathe deeply and calmly.

The element of Fire is connected with the suit of wands of the tarot.

Ideas connected with Fire:

Creativity

Divine spark

Innovation

Passion

Lust

Ingenuity

Destruction

Rebirth

Health

Some magical creatures associated with Fire are the djinn, salamanders, the phoenix, and the dragon. When drawing your circle, you can light an additional candle and some favorite spiced treats in a dish, such as candied ginger, black licorice, and cinnamon discs to call upon a fire guardian to watch over you while you work and keep you safe. When you invite the being, always say "Come to my humble circle in perfect love and perfect trust."

On your altar: To represent the element of Fire on your altar, light a candle in a suitable color for the moment. If open flames are not permitted, an LED candle or other sources of appealing light may be used. Additionally, a statue or figure of a fiery magical creature can take a candle's place.

Water

The element of Water represents emotion and memory. The depths of the ocean are too vast for us to yet understand, though we are drawn to the edge of the sea as if it were our mother—and it is. Yemaya calls to us to reach out for her; our ancestors reach for us from beyond the veil, encouraging us to understand our ancestral memories and our emotions.

Emotions can be frightening, just as water runs deep. The Water element in its quiet way dares us to be brave. Water nourishes us; without it, we could not survive. Additionally, Water represents movement as boats navigate rivers and oceans. Psychic dreams are also connected to Water.

Water is also powerful—both aggressively and passively. A mighty storm rolling off the ocean can level a city, and a steadily moving stream can, over eons, carve mountains. The Water element represents power both covert and overt—it is relentless, and it is patient.

The element of Water is connected with the suit of cups of the tarot.

Ideas connected with Fire:

Healing

Nourishment

Dreams

Emotions

Psychic abilities

Connection to other lives

Purification

Adaptability

Resilience

Beauty

Raw Power

Patience

Some magical creatures associated with Water are dryads, selkies, encantado, and undines. Do whatever you can to keep the bodies of water near you safe and clean. Consider volunteering with a river-keepers club. Also, provide places outside your home where creatures can get a drink on a dry day. A dish of marbles and water helps bees stay hydrated without risking drowning.

Before entering a body of water to swim, say a quiet prayer of thanks to the magical creatures who may be living there.

On your altar: To represent the element of Water, a dish or goblet of water is best. Stones such as aquamarine and clear quartz may also be used.

Finding Your Own Path

Embarking on a path of faith is about discovering yourself. The answers to who you are can be found both within your DNA, as well as scattered throughout the natural world. Wicca can help you connect with **you** by building a connection with the god and goddess. In our subconscious minds, we speak in a very different language—almost childlike, and full of wonder. Magic and meditation help us unlock the cipher our deeper selves have used to lend us clues: when we see a certain bird or animal during our day or notice a particular flower or stray feather on the wind, we can interpret these subtle messages from ourselves to discover answers to life's questions. Magic is both a homecoming and a new adventure—just as life begins again after death, so does the master become the pupil for another life's lessons.

You may feel overwhelmed at first as a novice drawn to Wicca but know that there is no rush, and no hurry. Traditional schools of witchcraft (such as Gardnerian, mentioned earlier) are not a fast-track way to knowledge; in fact, it is quite the opposite. Learning takes time and great patience, much as it did in older times when apprentices studied under the watchful eyes of their masters for a decade, and the first year or two merely involved sweeping up and keeping the workroom tidy.

Understand that being Wiccan is a way of life. It is, at first, a quiet practice, and it begins with a humble desire to know more than you do right now. If you are looking for an easy way to gain power, then perhaps, you should keep looking. True power comes from restraint, responsibility, knowing that force is only used when absolutely necessary, and most importantly—**that all actions have a reaction.** Magic comes with consequences.

Learn to Listen

A good rule of practice is to begin to grasp the art of being still, and listening. Daily meditation—a mere ten minutes a day—can help you hear the inner callings of your magical spirit. You may be overwhelmed by all of the choices available to you as a novice Wiccan. Whom should you pray to? There are so many deities to choose from. Being drawn to a god or goddess is more a mutual choice—two voices calling to one another in the darkness, then meeting up and becoming a combined source of light. This can take time, and you need not feel the urge to rush.

Keeping a journal of your daily observances can be helpful. What draws your eye the most when you are out in the natural world? What favorite things captivate you now? Such lists might look like this:

Favorite things	Seen today	Goals
crystals	a male cardinal	more energy
thunderstorms	a sunshower	to get stronger
kayaking	a rainbow trout	to be more successful at work
summer	a dream about	understanding and empathy
a flying serpent		

When you have filled a good portion of your list, fold it up and place it beneath a candle on your altar. Start a fresh list. At the coming of the next Sabbath or solstice, have a look at your first list and see if you can make any connections. What does the list say about you? What kind of witch will you be? What are your strengths? What areas of life are you most curious about?

Journaling, meditation, and reading are your greatest tools. The more you open your mind, the more open you will be to secrets revealed, over time.

Chapter 9 Tools of wiccan ritual: the athame

The Wiccan athame is a twofold edged ritual knife and is used for coordinating energy, for example, "cutting" undesirable vigorous ties, drawing images in the air, bringing the sacred circle before ritual and shutting it subsequently. The athame isn't extremely sharp, both for security reasons and because traditionally, it doesn't cut anything on the physical plane. The athame's manly, decisive characteristics make it an incredible portrayal of God.

Basic debate

The athame is related with both Fire and Air, contingent upon the tradition. The individuals who connect it with Air are drawing from the imagery of pre-Wiccan elusive frameworks like that found in the Hermetic Order of the Golden Dawn, which was a significant effect on Wicca. Because sharpness is related to keenness—the area of Air—and because the athame coordinates energy through its developments in the air, this affiliation feels the most valid for some Wiccans.

The individuals who connect it with a flame point to the way that blades are truly forged in flame, and that they are specialists of transformation. (Obviously, the last can be said about the wand also.) If you are a diverse expert without a set tradition to pursue, go with the affiliation that bodes well for you.

APPEARANCE

The quintessential athame takes after an essential knife. It has a dark grip, or handle, and is generally no longer than the length of one's hand. (A long knife can be clumsy and therefore dangerous, also more challenging to store and additionally travel with.) The handle is said to save a modest quantity of the supernatural energy brought up in ritual for later use, for example, in spellwork or charging different tools.

Athames can be found in shops gaining practical experience in Wicca and other "neopagan" spiritual traditions. Some have gorgeously ornate handles cut with abstract images or potentially set with gems. Others even have gem cutting edges. Without a doubt, an athame can be the most beautiful knife you've at any point seen!

In any case, not all Wiccans prefer or can afford the more glamorous forms, and many will bless an essential kitchen knife. You can draw your emblematic carvings into the handle if you go this course (being certain to wrap the cutting edge safely first!), but at the same time, it's fine to have a plain athame.

TO CUT OR NOT TO CUT

Although the athame is never used for real cutting in orthodox Wicca, more up to date traditions make a couple of special cases. These incorporate reaping herbs used in spellwork, forming another wand from the part of a tree, and cutting otherworldly images into a flame for ritual use.

Some kitchen Witches may even use their athame to get ready supernatural sustenances, in which case they will use a more down to earth, single-edged knife. Be that as it may, numerous experts use a different knife, called a boline, for these purposes. The boline is traditionally white-took care of, and keeping in mind that still viewed as a supernatural tool isn't used in genuine ritual.

PICKING YOUR ATHAME

Similarly, as with some other ritual tool, the way toward picking one can be intriguing and fun. If you're in a coven, at that point, you'll pick one that fits the coven's necessities. If you're singular, you have more choices. In any condition, make sure to take a couple of minutes with each knife you're thinking about, and observe how it feels in your grasp. You may need to get a few before you locate the one that is directly for you, however when you do discover it, you'll know it.

TOOLS OF WICCAN RITUAL: THE BELL

The use of bells is found in numerous religions other than Wicca, including Buddhism, Hinduism, Japanese Shinto, and numerous groups of Christianity. While the purpose and importance of bells change broadly among these different traditions, it's generally perceived that the ringing of a bell conveys a message or the like, regardless of whether to members in the religion or elements in the soul world. It's for this second purpose the bell is used in Wicca. A few people allude to it as a "witch's bell" to recognize it from bells used for different purposes. A better old term, you may run over is "demon driver."

The unmistakable, mending tone of a bell can have a couple of different impacts. The bell's vibrations can exile undesirable spirits as well as negative energies, bring in positive, wanted vigorous effects, or potentially basically bright dormant energy in any space all through one's home. Sound influences energy on a physical level—because the sound is energy—thus the bell is both a physical and an emblematic tool in Wiccan practice.

A PLETHORA OF USES

Not every single Wiccan tradition believe the bell to be a core ritual tool. Some may use it essentially for clearing the space before the ritual starts. Others use one to clear or potentially charge precious stones, herbs, and different things used in ritual and spellwork. Notwithstanding, numerous experts keep a bell on their altar and use it in their formal rituals. For this situation, the bell is ordinarily on the left half of the altar, where tools speaking to the Goddess are found. In many traditions, it is related to the component of Air, however some credit it to Water because of how sound waves swell outward when the bell is rung.

In ritual, the bell might be used to conjure the Goddess, as well as the Elements. Some will ring it in the wake of throwing the circle to seal the energy inside, while others will ring it in the wake of discharging the circle to scatter any residual energy. It can likewise be used to stamp different segments of a more extended ritual, for example, the part of the arrangement the start of the fundamental body of the ritual. Bells additionally make an exquisite method to seal different sorts of spellwork. Outside of ritual, numerous Wiccans like to balance one on the front door to protect their home.

DISCOVERING YOUR BELL

Similarly, as with each other ritual tool, you can discover a witch's bell in an assortment of Wiccan or potentially New Age shops. They run in appearance from plain and easy to ornately decorated. The primary thought, in any case, ought to be the bell's sound, which is why it's optimal to look for one face to face as opposed to online to make sure you're content with the tone. If you should buy one on the web, make certain to focus on the weight in the thing portrayal. While more massive bells might be more costly to deliver, lighter bells might not have the impact you want.

When you secure your ringer, invest some energy grasping it and focus on the physical sensations in your body as you do as such. At that point ring it tenderly and note how your energy changes. Use this tangible data to direct you as you choose how and when to use it in ritual and enchantment. The chime is one tool that will genuinely "talk" to you if you are happy to calm your brain and tune in!

TOOLS OF WICCAN RITUAL: THE BOLINE

You may as of now be acquainted with the ritual knife referred to in Wicca as the athame. While a few experts use the athame for all business related to ritual and enchantment, many don't use it to cut anything physical. Instead, they will keep a different knife for hacking herbs for spellwork, cutting supernatural strings and strips, cutting images into candles or various tools, as well as molding a wand cut from a tree limb. This knife, more down to earth yet no less sacred than the athame, is known as a boline.

The boline is generally white-took care of knife which, not at all like the run of the mill athame, is single-bladed and kept sharp for powerful cutting. The sharp edge might be straight or blow-molded. The bow shape, which can be followed back to medieval effects on stylized enchantment, can be perfect for collecting herbs, yet is to some degree less viable for cutting and cutting.

Similarly, as with the athame, you can discover resplendently cut and adorned bowlines in New Age shops with a Wiccan center, or you can get a basic one from any store selling kitchen supplies. You can likewise, obviously, repurpose a knife that you as of now have. Some Wiccan customs hold that any knife that has been used to cut creature tissue would not be suitable for a boline, yet this is an individual decision for each professional. If you put your knife through legitimate and exhaustive energy purifying, it may not make any difference for you what the knife was used for beforehand.

Regardless of where your boline originates from, make sure not to use it for any purposes outside of ritual and enchantment. Although it isn't used in formal Wiccan ritual, it's still prescribed to store your boline with your different tools, instead of in your flatware cabinet, to keep its mysterious energy undiluted between uses. For included security during storage, it's a smart thought to use a sheath or a thick fabric to envelop the edge by. Taking these measures will improve your fiery association with this most reasonable of otherworldly tools.

TOOLS OF WICCAN RITUAL: THE BROOM (BESOM)

Maybe the most common (and commonly misunderstood) image of Witches and Witchcraft in pop culture, the broom has been a piece of agnostic custom around the globe for quite a long time and has a fondness with present-day Wiccan practices. It's misty exactly how Witches flying around on broomsticks started, yet numerous individuals accept this to be a mixed-up translation of astral projection, which a few Witches in past hundreds of years would use psychoactive herbs to encourage. Here and there called "flying salves," these mixtures were likely the wellspring of the perplexity. How the broom turned into the vehicle in this image is as yet hazy, however the faith in flying Witches returns in any event to the extent the Middle Ages.

PURIFYING YOUR SPACE WITH THE BROOM

Generally called a "besom" and frequently high quality from the part of a tree, the broom isn't viewed as a center ritual tool in Wicca. However, it is regularly used to purify the ritual space before throwing the sacred circle. This doesn't normally include real clearing. However—the fibers of the besom by and large don't touch the floor. This is, even more, a ritual, vivacious purifying of the space, expelling negative energy or out and out enthusiastic "mess." This progression occurs after a decent unremarkable clearing with a standard broom (or vacuum) has effectively happened. Because ritual brooms fill in as purifiers, they are related to the component of Water and are in this way sacred to the Goddess.

The broom can likewise be used to help close the hover toward the part of the bargain. It very well may be profoundly viable at disseminating remaining energies raised during the ritual. During the ritual itself, the broom will, for the most part, sit to the side of the Wiccan special raised area. Something else, it's entirely expected to put it close to the passage to your home, to make preparations for negative or undesirable energy.

DISCOVERING YOUR BESOM

Ritual brooms can be any size, from smaller than expected "brightening" brooms that you here and there find in art stores or holding tight the divider in kitchens, to full-sized utilitarian brooms. Conventional woods used for sacred brooms incorporate birch, slag, and willow, however, any wood will do the trick. You can even discover directions for how to make your besom utilizing the sort of wood accessible in your general vicinity. A few Witches keep it straightforward by simply using a fallen tree limb as an emblematic broom.

Your broom doesn't need to be carefully assembled—common household brooms can likewise be committed to crafted by Witchcraft. However, it ought to in a perfect world have a wooden handle as opposed to metal or plastic. Regardless of what your broom is made of, however, it ought to never be used for ordinary housecleaning, as this would sully the sacred energy it holds for ritual and mystical purposes. This is one tool that ought not to be "repurposed" for enchantment, so plan to gain another broom of some sort, instead of endeavoring to sanctify an effectively used broom from your corridor storage room!

TOOLS OF WICCAN RITUAL: THE CAULDRON

Besde the sweeper and the wand, the cauldron is potentially the most iconic symbol of the Witch in the symbolism of popular culture. The birthplaces of this affiliation come to us from old Celtic legend, where cauldrons show up regarding numerous magical changes. Specifically, a few stories include a god known as the Dagda, who had a magic cauldron that was continually flooding with sustenance and would never be exhausted.

When it comes to Wiccan traditions, the cauldron is a symbol or indicative of the inventive powers of change. The round shape and responsive properties of cauldrons make it sacrosanct to the Goddess, and it is consistently connected with the element of Water. Nonetheless, given that the warmth of a fire is vital for a great part of the transformative work of a cauldron, some view it as offering relationship to both Water and Fire.

PRESENT-DAY USES FOR AN ANCIENT TOOL

The cauldron is not viewed as urgent to Wiccan ritual. In any case, it's incredible for magical work, as it tends to be used for fire spells as well as a spot to permit explain candles to consume securely, and can hold magically charged elements for elixir making. (While a few Witches may blend a magical mixture directly in the cauldron, the down to earth limitations of lighting a safe indoor fire underneath it will in general limit this use—regularly, the "fermenting" part of the magic is symbolic as opposed to exacting.)

Cauldrons can likewise fill in as a scrying tool when loaded up with new water and can be used in ritual to sub for the chalice, or to fill in as a holder for loose incense consumed on charcoal.

FINDING A CAULDRON

As you may have speculated, cauldrons are not the most straightforward of magical tools to stopped by—at any rate not since the development of power and kitchen stoves! Nonetheless, they are sold in some magical shops, and however they can be on the expensive side, they're incredible speculation for the individuals who need to fuse an old Witchy tradition into their training.

Cauldrons can be anyplace from a couple of crawls to a couple of feet crosswise over in the distance across; however, bigger sizes might be viewed as unrealistic except if you have yard space to set up your cauldron in. (All things considered, they're incredible for open-air ritual and spellwork!) If you're hoping to use your cauldron on your special stepped area, it's ideal to go with a little size. Most cauldrons lay on three legs, with the opening having a littler measurement than the largest piece of the bowl. Cast iron is viewed as the cauldron's optimal material; however, different metals are frequently used also.

If you can't discover (or manage) a cauldron, don't despair. A straightforward bowl can generally remain in the cauldron's place symbolically, and if it's warmth confirmation, can even be used for a portion of similar purposes.

TOOLS OF WICCAN RITUAL: THE CHALICE

Additionally, alluded to as the flagon in certain traditions, or, all the more just, the cup, the chalice speaks to the Goddess and the element of Water. It is a symbol of wealth and richness, and has a few purposes in Wiccan ritual, including offering drinks to the gods and sharing in the cakes and beer function. The chalice may hold water, wine or lager, contingent upon the ritual. It might likewise stand void in certain rituals, as a symbol of opening oneself to the bounty pouring forward from the spiritual plane. (Note: in any ritual requiring a mixed drink, juice or natural tea might be used as a substitute.)

Traditionally, the chalice is silver, a shading (and metal) consecrated to the Goddess. This kind of chalice can be found at shops having some expertise in Wicca and additionally other "neopagan" traditions. In any case, these can be costly and relying upon the quality, possibly poisonous to drink from. Wine specifically can erode metal, so if you're utilizing a metal-plated chalice, use a different drinks cup for wine or other acidic refreshments.

A rich silver chalice can be stunning to work with, yet it's positively a bit much. You can discover something more straightforward and more affordable, or even devote a cup you effectively claim for a reason. It tends to be especially amazing to use one that has been in your family for quite a while, as it will have many adoring vibrations stockpiled in it as of now. Flagon shaped cups or short-stemmed wine glasses are pleasant, yet anything that holds fluid will do. Wood, clay, metal, or glass are suitable materials. Plastic, then again, isn't suggested, as it's anything but an Earth-sourced material.

Regardless of what vessel you pick as your chalice, make sure to keep it held exclusively for ritual purposes. Try not to hurl it in the dishwasher with the majority of your different cups. Wash it by hand, independently, and keep it with your other ritual tools. Along these lines, it will reliably hold the magical energy you have accused it of.

TOOLS OF WICCAN RITUAL: INCENSE

Found in numerous religions going back to the relic, incense is an old ritual tool that draws on the sweet-smelling forces of herbs, flavors, oils, saps, and tree rinds to make a hallowed climate and a perspective helpful for communing with the soul world. Speaking to the element of Air (and in certain traditions, the element of Fire), incense is viewed as a center segment of Wiccan ritual and is likewise regularly used as an extra to magic.

RITUAL TRADITIONS AND INCENSE MAGIC

The most traditional approach to use incense in ritual is to put a loose mix of dried herbs or potentially sap granules in a censer. The censer might be dangled from chains, similar to those used in the Catholic church, and bore the hover as it is thrown, as well as set to the other side of the Wiccan special raised area to consume all through the ritual procedures. Then again, a few Wiccans like to use a little cauldron as their censer, which harkens back to earlier hundreds of years.

Because loose incense can be to some degree work escalated— requiring charcoal and a warmth confirmation dish or the like—numerous individuals pick to use incense sticks or cones, which still require holders yet include less arrangement and a fairly lower danger of fire. If you're beginning, this more straightforward methodology might be simply the best approach, yet help out and attempt loose incense eventually in your training—its upgrade of ritual energy is very brilliant!

Notwithstanding consuming during the formal Wiccan ritual, incense is likewise used as an offering and might be set before pictures of gods in a changeless sanctuary. It is additionally frequently consumed during spellwork, as the scented smoke can encourage a perfect perspective—both focused and loose—for working fruitful magic. Moreover, most herbs, flavors, barks, and roots have specific magical characteristics, which can be coordinated with the end goal of the spellwork.

A few people likewise prefer to use the smoke from the incense as a kind of scrying tool, looking for pictures of the divinities being conjured in a ritual or other pictorial message that may come through. Contingent upon the specific elements of the incense, the smoke may likewise be used to purify ritual tools and other magical things.

WHICH INCENSE IS BEST FOR YOU?

A wide range of sorts of incense is winding up progressively broadly accessible, in New Age shops as well as in numerous different places too, including some supermarkets! A few brands consume more neatly than others, be that as it may. Continuously read the name on any incense you're thinking about buying and watch out for any engineered aromas. Give the case a decent sniff before buying—although the smell of the smoke will be to some degree different from the smell of the incense itself, and you can wager that if you don't care for the aroma of the bundle, you won't care for what's inside!

Investigating new sorts of incense can be a brilliant method to keep your training dynamic long after you have the ritual "essentials" built up. In the end, you may even wish to make your very own incense utilizing your preferred fixings! Be that as it may, if you're profoundly delicate to the smoke of any sort, don't stress. You can use basic oils on candles or in a diffuser to make a fragrant comparative impact without activating sensitivities, asthma, or other medical problems. Whatever you pick, in any case, it's commonly concurred that some type of fragrant improvement is ideal for ritual and magical work. A couple of things have more effect on the lively state than a sense of smell!

TOOLS OF WICCAN RITUAL: THE PENTACLE

In fact, talking, a pentacle is a plate-shaped section with at least one magical symbol inscribed in it. Most regularly, and particularly in Wicca, pentacles are inscribed with a pentagram—the upstanding five-pointed star—with a hover around it (making the name "pentacle" rather consummately proper!).

The five-pointed star is an old symbol, found in both Eastern and Western cultures, and has been used to speak to different parts of human and spiritual concerns. As an Earth-related symbol, it is related in great Tarot decks with plenitude. Its use in Wicca originates from traditions of ceremonial magic. Each point is said to speak to the elements of Air, Earth, Fire, and Water, with the fifth element (Spirit) as the upward point. Its round shape and Earth affiliations make it consecrated to the Goddess.

PRAGMATIC PENTACLE MAGIC

As a symbol, the pentagram is considered to have innate magical powers and is regularly inscribed on objects, for example, the grip of an athame or the front of a Book of Shadows. This shape has attracted the air during certain rituals, either with an athame or wand, to add capacity to the work. It is additionally viewed as an indication of assurance from negative or hurtful energies.

As an object, the pentacle section is regularly used to charge elements for spellwork. Starting sanctification of ritual tools is additionally performed by laying the tool on a pentacle. They may show these transparently or keep them tucked under their garments, contingent upon whether they wish to pronounce their spiritual character to everyone around them.

GETTING A PENTACLE

It would be very uncommon for "Another Age" shop with any Wiccan leanings at all to not convey some pentacle. They are frequently made of pewter or other metal, yet can likewise be made of wood, stone, mud, or even wax. Some are complicatedly cut or potentially set with semiprecious gemstones, while others are very straightforward. A pentacle can be any size, however you by and large need one little enough to fit serenely on the particular raised area with the other ritual tools. If you discover one containing different symbols past the pentagram itself, it's a smart thought to realize a big motivator for them before bringing the object into your ritual work. A pentacle is a powerful tool in your training, so it's imperative to make sure it's a solid match with your very own energy.

Obviously, like most other ritual tools, you can make your very own pentacle. If you have a round level object of any sort—a drink liner, a container top, and so on.— And a conventional hand with drawing or painting, there's no reason not to create your own. You can even discover layouts online for following an ideal pentacle. Make sure to place your very own positive energy into the majority of the materials previously and during the creation procedure!

TOOLS OF WICCAN RITUAL: THE WAND

Like the floor brush and the cauldron, the wand is an iconic symbol of Witches in fairy stories and contemporary culture the same. Used in religious and magical customs going back to the antiquated Egyptians, the wand came into use in Wiccan ritual through the impact of ceremonial magic.

Obviously, notwithstanding every one of the portrayals in popular culture, it isn't the wand that causes magical change, however the specialist, who accuses the wand of individual power. Like the athame, it is used to coordinate energy, however in a to some degree progressively unobtrusive, delicate way than the swiftly conclusive knife. The wand is regularly used in Wiccan ritual to conjure the Goddess and

God and might be used to attract magical symbols the air or on the ground. It can likewise be used to draw the hover inside which the ritual or spellwork is performed.

Likewise, like the athame, the wand is a direct, projective shape, as is additionally consecrated to God. The wand is related to the element of Air in certain traditions, because of its relationship with trees and because it is frequently waved in the air. Different traditions partner it with Fire because it is traditionally observed as an operator of change. Regardless of whether you attribute the wand to Fire and the athame to Air, or the other way around, will rely upon the tradition you're following. If you're rehearsing as a singular mixed, at that point go with what feels right to you.

FINDING YOUR WAND

Wands can be any length under 12 inches or somewhere in the vicinity—about the length of your lower arm or shorter—and can be made of different materials. There are some beautiful wands accessible at Wiccan or "New Age" shops made from glass or pewter, with elaborate carvings and gem focus joined to the closures, and even short wands made from a tight length of the cleaned gemstone.

Nonetheless, the wand is traditionally made of wood, particularly from oak, hazel, senior, and willow trees, and numerous Wiccans lean toward their wands to be as near Nature as could be expected under the circumstances. You can locate these progressively "provincial" wands accessible for buy too, but at the same time, it's a good thought to go out and locate your own!

If you approach a lush territory, or even only a tree in your lawn, you can wander out with your intuition honed and prepared to sense only the tree, and simply the branch, where your wand is hanging tight for you. Watch out for fallen branches or twigs on the ground around the tree, as it's desirable over reaping them that way, instead of cutting into a living tree.

If you do feel called to assemble a live branch, ask authorization from the tree and hold up until you feel a positive reaction from your higher self. If this doesn't occur or you get a negative inclination, proceed onward to a different tree. Use your boline or another knife that you've rinsed and blessed for this reason. Make sure to thank the tree for offering its energy to you as you recover your new wand. It's great to bring along a little offering—a touch of herbs, milk, or nectar—to leave at the base of the storage compartment.

URBAN OPTIONS

If, in the same way as other, you don't approach much in the method for a forest or timberland, at that point consider acquiring a wooden dowel from a specialty store. These, similar to branches you discover outside, might be designed any way you like. You can cut symbols, join gemstones to the tip, envelop the base by strip, or apply stain to obscure the shading.

Numerous individuals accept that hand-made wands, made by the individual who will use it, are more dominant than locally acquired wands. Toward the day's end, be that as it may, it's up to you. So be patient and use your instinct, and the correct wand will introduce itself to you when you are prepared.

Clearing and charging magical ingredients and ritual tools

Enchantment is about energy—your energy, the energy of the Universe, the energy of the gods, elementals, guides, and other non-physical elements you may work with, and the energy of the aim you're working enchantment for. It pursues, at that point, that the energy of the physical tools you work with is a significant factor in the accomplishment of your enchantment, just as the nature of any customs and rituals you execute as a major aspect of your Wiccan practice. Therefore, it's imperative to clear new ritual tools and spell ingredients of any unwanted lingering energy, and after that, accuse them of purposeful, positive energy before utilizing them in ritual or spellwork.

CLEARING: OUT WITH THE OLD

Unwanted energy can emerge out of a wide range of spots, notwithstanding when it comes to fresh out of the plastic new ritual tools. The way toward assembling, shipping, and after that selling pretty much any item, regardless of whether it's a light or a cauldron, includes the energy of different individuals who handle the item en route. If you get something used, at that point there's significantly more grounded energy present in the item, from its past owner(s). Have you at any point gotten an item of clothing or a book in a thrift store and felt your state of mind change as you grasped it? That is another person's unwanted energy!

There's no should fear extra, unwanted, or "remote" energy when it goes to your ritual tools and magical items. It's everything simply vigorous mess that can be cleaned up like residue from the furniture. Be that as it may, the clearing step is a significant one if you need a "without static" association with the non-physical plane through these specific objects.

So how would you clear unwanted energy? There are a few different techniques, and some are more qualified for specific items than others. For instance, ocean salt is a reliable chemical of denser energies, especially when it comes to gems and candles. It works by ingestion—cover the item in a bowl of salt and leave for a few hours or medium-term, at that point expel and flush. (Make sure to discard the salt.) A minor departure from this strategy is to disintegrate ocean salt in water and splash or sprinkle your objects. In any case, contingent upon their specific piece, not all items hold up well in a salt shower, so do some examination first.

Daylight is another common purifying specialist. Spread your ritual tools out in direct daylight for in any event one hour, and any unwanted energy will be consumed with extreme heat, leaving them purified and prepared to be accused of your very own energy for most significant impact. Evening glow works a similar way and is ideal for any items that may be blurred or generally hurt by the light and warmth from the Sun. This is particularly material to specific gems and herbs you might need to use in spellwork.

Smirching with sage, rosemary, lavender, and additionally other purging herbs is an old custom practiced by shamanic people groups the world over. It works to get out unwanted energy from objects, physical spaces, and even individuals. Sound is another incredible way to separate and scatter stale energy—have a go at ringing a ringer or a few tolls over your progressively sensitive ritual tools and ingredients to clear them for magical use.

CHARGING: IN WITH THE NEW

The subsequent stage in setting up your ritual tools and spellwork items is accusing them of the energy of your personal goal for their utilization. For instance, you may accuse a precious citrine stone of glad, sure energy with the goal that this vibration will be accessible to you whenever you have to approach it by grasping the stone. If you're charging a flame for a specific spell, you'll center around the association between the light and the objective you're working on manifesting.

Both daylight and twilight twofold as charging specialists, so you can basically clear and charge simultaneously. Make sure, if you're charging for a specific objective, that you center that expectation into the item when you spread it out under your preferred heavenly body. Another essential technique is to lay your object on a pentacle chunk (which has just been cleared and charged). For an extra "support," lay the pentacle in daylight or evening glow. Amethyst and quartz precious stones are likewise phenomenal chargers in their very own right, so you can put herbs, littler stones, ritual gems, or whatever other objects that will fit right onto these shining marvels.

Regardless of which technique you use, the energy of your own engaged goal is the way into the procedure. Imagine the result you're looking for when you charge your ritual tools and magical ingredients. Material association—grasping the object or putting your fingers on it while it lays on a surface—is a decent way to move your capacity to it. Talking expressions of goal can genuinely enable you to sharpen your center, so think of certain words that express your longing here. For instance, when charging for a specific spell, you may state:

"You charge this [name the object]

Through the Universal power

To bring [name the magical purpose]

Into your life.

So, let it be."

SANCTIFYING YOUR RITUAL TOOLS

When it comes to ritual tools, for example, your wand or athame, accusing is commonly consolidated of what we call "sanctification." Consecration ordinarily includes conjuring the God and Goddess as well as the Elements as a way of associating the ritual objects legitimately with the celestial. Contingent upon how you approach your practice, this might be a more intricate procedure than that utilized for charging spell ingredients. Regularly individuals will cast a hover for this work, or else join the charging of new items into a more significant ritual. Special raised area tools are customarily sanctified on a pentacle, or a pentacle may be drawn with a wand or athame over the object in the focal point of the raised area. If you're new to the Wiccan practice, you should attempt a couple of different ways to deal with find what feels most dominant and valid for you.

It might feel now and again, like clearing and charging your tools and ingredients is an issue. Be that as it may, it's always justified, despite all the trouble to set aside the effort to play out these means. Not exclusively is simply the energy of the objects significantly better, yet ground-breaking enthusiastic changes happen inside you as you center around your practice along these lines. If you genuinely need to comprehend the difference, attempt a spell without charging your ingredients first, and afterward try a similar spell again with charged ingredients. You'll be stunned at exactly how genuine this "energy" business is!

Chapter 10 Wiccan clothing and ritual attire

Many hopeful Wiccans wind up pondering whether there's hugely a "clothing regulation" for taking an interest in formal rituals. Much has been made of the practice of working "skyclad," or naked, in Wiccan covens. While the facts confirm that the first Gardnerian type of Witchcraft included ritual nakedness and that numerous conventional covens still pursue this practice, skyclad is surely not by any means the only choice. Today there are numerous inventive, mixed ways to deal with Wiccan clothing and gems, as you will see beneath.

If you're trying to join a coven or a casual Wiccan circle, you'll need to discover what their conventions are as far as ritual attire (if any) and decide to what you're OK with. If you're a singular Wiccan, you don't have to check with anybody, however yourself when it comes to what you'll wear during the ritual. If you pursue a custom that calls for working skyclad as alone and you're alright with it, by all methods do! Else, you might need to consider some other normal choices utilized by covens, circles, and solitaries the same.

ROBES, CLOAKS, AND OTHER POSSIBILITIES

COMMON WICCAN CLOTHING ITEMS

Wiccans and different Pagans regularly wear ritual robes as a way of isolating themselves from the ordinary commonplace parts of life and upgrading their feeling of enchantment and riddle. For these professionals, wearing a robe is as much a piece of the psychological and spiritual arrangement for ritual as cleaning up or sitting in contemplation. Regularly Wiccans wear nothing underneath their ritual robes, yet this is a personal decision—as always, do what's agreeable for you.

Robes can be acquired or high quality—you can discover straightforward examples online regardless of whether you're not an accomplished sewer—and are accessible in pretty much every shading possible. Irrespective of whether you're purchasing or sewing, notwithstanding, make sure to focus on a significant thought: combustibility. There are some intricate and streaming robe structures out there that ought not to be worn anyplace close to light fire, particularly if there's a breeze!

A few professionals want to wear a shroud during the ritual, especially if it's being held outside. These can be put on over ritual robes or normal clothing, however, are commonly not worn without anyone else since they generally affix at the neck. Contingent upon how to expand the structure, shrouds could conceivably have hoods as well as sleeves. Similarly, as with robes, you can discover a lot of pre-made shrouds on the web, or make your own. You could likewise do some chasing around at vintage shops and repurpose an old article of clothing into your ritual shroud!

There's no need, be that as it may, to make or buy unique Wiccan clothing for your ritual work if you're a single professional. A lot of Wiccans wear something that is as of now significant to them—a most loved flowy dress or shirt, an all-dark group, or some different bits of clothing that has a different reverberation.

WICCAN JEWELRY

Notwithstanding, or even rather than, exceptional clothing, numerous Wiccans will wear at least one bits of magical gems during ritual and spellwork. This may incorporate a pentacle or other magical image on a string or chain around the neck; precious stone-studded rings, armlets, anklets or pieces of jewelry; or even a diamond-encrusted headpiece. Anything that you feel upgrades your energy is a decent decision.

It's ideal for accusing these bits of your power to get the perfect impact. If you charge them well, with enough engaged aim, you will probably feel a slight "buzz" of energy when you put them on.

Chapter 11 Wicca Goddess and Gods

The religion of Wicca portrays Nature as created and driven by two main forces: the masculine God and the feminine Goddess. The Goddess and the God are the creators of all physical and spiritual reality, both seen and unseen existence. They are together to bring balance to all life and one cannot exist without the other.

As part of Nature, we all have a spark of both energies within us. Practitioners of Wicca do not wait for special dates or occasions to perform a ritual in order to connect with their God and Goddess.

For instance, being mindful of the natural scenery that surrounds you, the plants, the mountains, and animals, watching the Sun rise and set, watching the Moon are all considered rituals in and of themselves. Wiccans are aware of the presence of God and Goddess in everything that surrounds us.

In the religion of Wicca, Gods and Goddesses have been given many names, however, some are called Nameless.

You have probably heard of some of the Goddesses names like Aphrodite, Diana, Freya, Gaia, Inanna and Nut/Nuit, some of the more frequently used God names are Pan, Eros, Apollo, Horus, Osiris, Ra, and Thorus. You recognized some of the names mentioned so far as the same names present in Greek and Egyptian religion and history. Wicca followers see their Gods and Goddesses in any and all forms they are comfortable with, as the Divine is all around us. They watch the Sun and thank their God for all the life they have received on this world.

In Wicca, the Goddess is represented as Triple Goddess

This is a symbol of the three stages of life.

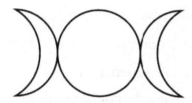

As Maiden - symbolized by the waxing moon represents the youth, tenderness and innocent young girl

Mother - symbolized by the full moon represents the mature, protective, nurturing woman in her motherhood stage.

The Crone - symbol is waning moon in a representation of the old woman, wise and great teacher full of knowledge.

Law of Threefold

The Wiccan Rede represents the ethical code of the people who follow the Wicca path. This is the Wicca version of 'The law of cause and effect'.

The term "Rede" originates from the old English word "roedan" which means to direct, or to lead. The Wiccan Law of three was written in the beginning of the 20th century by an unknown source.

Wicca teaches that we all send energy into the Universe with our words and actions, and whatever energy we sent out, we get it back threefold. Wiccans believe in the right to use their will and energy freely as long as it does not cause harm to another human being. The Law of Three has directs the physical, emotional and spiritual world of the follower. Wiccans believe that, ultimately, everyone is responsible for his or her actions and doings. Trying to gain power over other people and achieving your goals at the expense of someone else is strictly prohibited in Wicca. They do not worship nor believe in Satan and human sacrifices are not part of this religion. Those who practice black magic and try to gain power over other people, try to harm other people are not considered Wiccan.

Chapter 12 Sabbats and esbats

The Sabbats and Esbats are the actual events in Nature. Sabbats are based on the solar calendar and they celebrate The God and The Sun as the male energy of The All. Sabbats refer to the natural cycles of the Earth. There are eight Sabbats and they represent the equinoxes - the two days in the year when the day and the night are of equal duration, the longest and the shortest day of the year, the longest night of the year also known as the solstice and the midpoints between these natural manifestations.

The Sabbats which represent the midpoints between these four occurrences represent the peaks of the four seasons. They are called the major Sabbats.

Samhain: October 31

Also known as Halloween or the Witch's New Year. This is one of the most important holidays in Wicca, and it represents a major spiritual event. On this day they honor the dead, as it marks the death of the Lord. It is said that on this day the veil between the living and the dead is thinnest. On this day, they leave food out for loved ones who died.

Yule: December 21 Winter solstice

Represents the longest night of the year. The God is reborn again and the light is returned to Earth. They celebrate this holiday by exchanging gifts as a symbol for better future.

Imbolc: February 2

Also knows as Brigid's day-keeper of the sacred fire. Imbolc represents the peak of the winter, and it is celebrated through lighting fires and candles.

Ostara: March 21

Symbolizes the beginning of Spring, new life, and fertility. It holds the religious significance of Nature's rebirth and is considered as the time for new projects and personal development. Wiccans celebrate this with boiled eggs and blessings for a better future.

Beltane: May 1st

Represents the peak of Spring and is celebrated as the day when God and Goddess unite in a sacred marriage. Beltane is inspired by the rebirth of life, green nature, and blossoming of trees and flowers. It is a great day for bringing flowers to your home.

Summer Solstice: June 21: A midsummer

The start of the summer and the longest day of the year. This is a great period to perform healing magick, especially through outdoor rituals. Nature in this period is most abundant.

Lughnassad: August 2: First harvest

Characterizing the beginning of the full harvest, Lughnassad is also known as the Feast of Bread and is traditionally the day for baking bread. While performing rituals, Wiccans decorate their altar with fruits and vegetables.

Mabon: September 21 Harvest festival

The length of the day and the night is equal and it marks the approach of winter and darkness. During this time, Wiccans celebrate and give thanks to God for the abundance received that year.

Esbats

Esbats are Moon rituals through which Wicca celebrate the Goddess and the feminine energy. Esbats celebrations usually worship the full moon and it is believed that on the full moon the magickal powers of the Goddess are at their peak.

At least once a month Wiccans and Witches honor the Goddess by celebrating one of the three phases of the moon, depending on what kind of energy they need for themselves.

- New Moon

Wiccans perform rituals on new moon when they need a new beginning, a fresh start in their lives.

- The Waxing Moon

This is the time of the year when the illuminated part of the moon is growing bigger and brighter. It is considered the ideal time to gain more positivity and strength in your life for all the new goals you've set for yourself under the new moon.

-The Full Moon

This is the time when Moon's energy is at its peak. This is the time to cast your spells and go for what you truly want. The three days before and after the Full Moon are considered a period of great power and influence as the night of the full moon.

-The Waning Moon

This is the period when the moon is getting smaller and it represents the perfect time to get rid of all the negativity in your life. This negativity can come in any shape or form; however, it is important to note that no one must be harmed in this process.

A solar year has 13 full moons, the 29.5-day lunar cycle 1, a year has one full moon per month plus one extra called the Blue Moon.

January: Wolf Moon

This is the time for self - evaluation. See yourself as a seed that has been planted and is waiting for the spring to be born again.

February: Storm Moon

A perfect time to get rid of any negativity. The full moon signifies self - forgiveness, mental house cleaning, and self - purification.

March: Chaste Moon

A great time for new beginnings and to start working on the projects you planned last fall and set your ideas to cultivate.

April: Seed Moon

It is time for fertility, wisdom, and growth. A perfect time to saw the seeds of your magick. Move from planning into action.

May: Hare Moon

A celebration of health, life, romance and loving relationships. Great time to embrace your true self and make some time living your own passion.

June: Dryad Moon

Known as Strawberry Moon, it represents the Lover's full moon that gives energy for love, marriage and success. A time to nurture your inner garden.

July: Mead Moon

A great time for meditation, dream work and prosperity. Performing magick in this period of the year is an especially sublime experience.

August: Wyrt Moon

Perfect time to reap the benefits from your magick work and thank the God and the Goddess for the abundance received, crafts and ambition.

September: Harvest Moon

Time for protection and prosperity. A perfect time to reorganize your spiritual and emotional state from summer.

October: Blood Moon

Use the moon's energies for setting new goals, enhance your spiritual life, meditate on death and rebirth and think about reincarnation.

November: Snow Moon

A good time to work on yourself, to reduce stress and to gain strength for your relationships with others.

December: Oak Moon

It is the last full moon of the year. Plan what you want to achieve for the next year and ask Goddess for guidance.

Chapter 13 Healing spells

In a similar fashion to spells of protection, there are a great number of spells which are focused on the healing and the betterment of the human body. As a powerful conduit for witchcraft and magic, the importance of good health in Wicca is often underestimated, so being able to cleanse and heal oneself is vital. However, as with many medical concerns, witchcraft such as that detailed below is not designed to replace the advice of a doctor, merely to complement it. You should always listen to the advice of medical professionals.

A spell for healing

This is a great spell for those who are trying to encourage a healing process in others. As a witch and a Wicca practitioner, you will often find that many people are interested in the kind of spiritual, energized healing that this kind of witchcraft is able to offer. Thanks to the power of magic, you can use spells such as these to help with the healing process.

The first thing that you will need to do is to encourage your patient to relax. Just as you yourself have entered into a meditative state in the previous spells which we have covered, you can now demonstrate your learning by encouraging someone to enter into a similarly relaxed mode. Slow the breathing, and allow yourself into what is known as a "neutral mode," in which you are both relaxed.

As you both begin to relax, you should feel the positive energies and warmth enter into the surrounding space. These might be spirits, goddesses, or whatever the various elements of your own personal brand of Wicca might involve. These are the spirits who will be helping you to heal. Encourage your patient to begin talking, expressing the various parts of their life which are positive. Whether it is relationships, their career, or anything else, encourage them to focus on the best aspects of their life, bringing these energies to the forefront.

Remain in a positive and happy state, eliciting these emotions from the patient. Have them close their eyes, and you do the same. As well as speaking aloud, the positive aspects and energies should begin to fill the room with a warmth and a strong healing aura. Once you are happy that these spirits are present and that they are positive, you should begin to encourage them to help with the healing.

Quietly so that your patient doesn't hear, begin to list the issues which are afflicting the patient and on which you wish the spirits to focus. During this time, the patient should be focusing on the positive aspects of their life and the things which they enjoy doing when they are at their most healthy.

If you have practiced the protective spells from earlier in this book, begin to create the positive shield using an aura of light.

Rather than limiting this to protecting yourself, however, imagine that the light is reaching out from beyond you and layering over the patient. This healing energy will be able to not only prevent negative energies from infiltrating your patient, it will also help remove the negative aspects that might be hindering the healing process.

Continue in this fashion. After five minutes, you and your patient should both begin to feel empowered and protected. Thanks to the layer of positivity that has descended over you both and the protective shield that has been created, the spirits that you have invoked should be able to help you with the healing process.

Once this is complete, begin to encourage you both out of the meditative state. Talk softly and guide your patient back into the room now that they have been cleansed and protected. If needed, you can repeat this process once a day in order to bring the best kind of positive energy to your patient's life.

As well as this healing process, the presence of nature in the patient's life is very much encouraged. It is not uncommon to find that many of those whose healing is slower than they might like have very little interaction with nature. This can be as much as adding a houseplant or two to their home or simply walking through a park. Try to suggest that they strengthen their bond with nature in as many ways as possible as this will boost the effectiveness of your own efforts.

A cleansing ritual with the power to heal

Just as a cleansing ritual can be used to protect against negative and untoward spirits, these kinds of rituals can also be used to help remove similar energies from the body and to assist with the healing process. When you are worried about an illness or are not feeling great, then it can often be helpful to ensure that you are correctly cleansed of these kinds of auras. In order to accomplish this, follow these steps. You will need:

- Incense to burn (sage, preferably)
- A single candle (ideally silver or grey-colored)
- A sprinkling of sea salt
- A chalice or cup filled with water (tap water is fine)

Respectively, these items represent the four traditional elements; earth, air, fire, and water. Place the candle in front of you in a quiet room and light the candle and the incense. Begin to settle into a meditative state and remember that the more relaxed you are, the more effective the spell becomes. For those who are feeling ill or under the weather, this can be a difficult step, but being able to temporarily overcome an illness can be rewarding in the long run.

As soon as you are feeling relaxed enough, you can begin.

As the incense begins to smolder and the scent fills the room, cast your hand through the smoke several times. Allow the smoke to pass over your skin and notice the smell as it fills the room. As you are doing so, say the following words:

"With air I cleanse myself."

Next, hold your hand over the burning candle (not close enough to hurt, but close enough to feel the heat on your palm) and say:

"With fire I cleanse myself."

As you say the words, begin to feel the negative energies and the illness burning and smoldering. Next, pick up a pinch of sea salt and rub it between your forefingers and thumb. Then rub the salt over the palm of each hand and say to yourself:

"With earth I cleanse myself."

Finally, dip your hands into the water and wash away the salt and the traces of sage incense. As you clean your hands, repeat these words:

"With water I cleanse myself."

As soon as this is complete, you can extinguish the candles with your still wet fingers and dry your hands. If done correctly, you should begin to feel the illness and the negative spirits departing over the coming days.

A spell for the release of negativity

If you are still encountering negative and harmful energies in your life, this can have an adverse effect on your health. In situations such as these, the most effective solution can sometimes be to simply ask the energies to leave. The power of Wicca is such that not only will it help you identify these energies, but it will also grant you the power to properly dismiss them from your life. If this is the kind of situation in which you find yourself, then read on to discover the best way in which to deal with these issues.

To complete the exercise you will need only a quiet room and a red candle. Turn off all of the lights and place the candle directly in front of you. As it is lit, begin to enter into a meditation. While you might normally close your eyes, you should instead leave them open and focus directly on the flame as it burns. As you consider the lit candle, focus on the power and the strength of fire as a general force. This is the kind of power that will grant you the ability to drive out the negativity.

Once you have become fixed on the idea of the fire, then you will need to say the following words out loud to the room:

"Any energy that no longer serves me,
please leave now.

Thank you for your presence.

Now I am sending you home."

The way in which you say the words will matter. You will need to fill your voice with conviction, concentrating on the power of the fire before you and turning this power into the tone with which you will drive out the negativity.

Repeat the words, driving them out to the room at large. It can help to visualize the negativity being removed from your body, peeling away like a snake shedding its skin. This is the healing process made real, helping you to find the right energy with which to heal yourself and drive out the unwanted energies.

As you proceed, you should feel yourself becoming lighter and lighter. Once this feeling begins to arrive, you may extinguish the candle and resume your day-to-day activities as you begin to heal.

A healing spell that uses light

We have already mentioned how powerful light is as a force and how it can be used to remove negative and harmful energies from your life. As the final step for those who are searching for a healing solution, light could well be the missing ingredient that you require in order to get the best results. For those who have conducted the previous healing steps, repairing the holes in your aura with light is very important, so read on to discover how it can be done.

Again, find a quiet place to sit and be sure that you will not be disturbed. Using the method of aura creation which we covered earlier, we will repair the holes and will begin with the top of your head. This is perhaps one of the most important areas of the body and will thus need to be healed as soon as possible. Visualize the light resting on your head as a crown, a display of strength which is bound on to the top of your head. Continue to hold this imagine and reach up and touch your head with delicate fingers.

In doing this, you will now need to stretch the healing light down over your body. As the powerful aura stretches over your body, it will begin to fill in any gaps and holes which have emerged and which could be causing you issues. Say the following words as you do so:

"I ask that my energy body is filled

with pure healing light."

Use these words several times until you feel confident that the healing process is correctly handled and that your aura has been repaired. Once complete, thank the spirits, the goddess, and the elements, and resume your day-to-day life. If you have been feeling ill, it can be helpful to repeat this process several times in order to better repair yourself while you are feeling at your worst.

An incantation for self-healing

Just as an awareness of the power of Wicca is important, turning this power on yourself can be a great way in which to heal general malaise and worry from about your person. For this particular incantation, you will be making use of ancient wisdom to make the most of the healing properties inherent in the art of Wicca.

More than others, this powerful spell is largely dependent on the abilities of the witch. Even if you do not consider yourself much more than a beginner, practicing and perfecting this spell can be essential if you wish to use Wicca to self-heal. As well as this, it can be best used in combination with modern medicine, exacerbating the effectiveness of the drugs which your doctor is able to provide.

The first thing that we will need to learn is this mantra. This collection of words has been passed down and has become known among many Wicca users to be one of the best ways in which to heal a body. Consider these words:

By Earth and Water,

Air and By Fire,

May you hear this wish,

Sources of Life and Light

Sources of the day and of the Earth,

I invoke you here,

Heal my body and mind.

Learn them by heart, and be sure to use them whenever you are feeling anything other than your best. The words will help to refocus your energies and drive the power of Wicca's energies to help heal the witch's body.

Bringing harmony and peace to an infected space

While it might seem that the body is the element most in need of healing when a person is ill, it can also be useful to heal spaces. By bringing harmony and peace to a room or home, you can accelerate the healing process and ensure that you have the best environment possible to recover.

It can even be used in outside spaces, though the effectiveness might be limited by both the power of the spell caster and the size of the space available. To carry out this incantation, you will require potted plants of the following herbs:

- Rosemary
- Thyme
- Cinnamon

If you cannot get access to these materials, dried herbs and a generic potted plant can be used though they will not be as powerful. The aim is to transfer the power of the spell into the living plants and to allow them to grow and flourish in the space that needs healing.

First, arrange the potted plants in front of you in a line. If you have just one pot, then place that directly in front of you, making sure that the soil is within reach of both hands. Cast your palms over each of the pots in turn (or over the dried herbs) and say the following words:

Balance and harmony,

Peacefulness and ease,

By the Power of Three

All turbulence ceases.

As you are saying the blessing, imagine the energies that you are able to generate as they flow into the plants. The living quality of the soil is becoming imbued with the healing energy that you are providing, which will in turn feed into the roots of the plant. Once complete, you should place the potted plant into the space that you wish to heal.

The spell will continue to work as long as the plant remains healthy and alive and as long as there is one person nearby who is able to occasionally reinforce the positive energies which are present. With these two factors, the plant should continue to provide a lasting healing help.

Distance Healing Spell

Our final healing spell is designed for use over longer distances. As you might imagine, projecting your power over a long distance can be more difficult than close quarter's magic. As well as this, discerning the results can be difficult, so do not be dismayed if you are not able to notice immediate results. Persist with the spell, and refine your abilities.

To complete this spell, you will need:

- Three large candles (white)
- A picture or image of the person who is in need of healing (the more recent, the better)
- A single crystal (preferably quartz)
- A selection of incenses of your choosing.

To begin, place the candles in a semi-circle (half-moon) in front of you. The incense should be lit, placed out of sight, and allowed to burn while you conduct the rest of the spell. Take a hold of the image of the patient and gently place it into the center of the semi-circle so that it is still facing toward you. Place the crystal on top of the picture.

Sit down. Place both of your hands flat against your thighs. Feel your weight moving down through your thighs, legs, and into the ground. Center your weight so that there is a sense of oneness with the ground and the rest of the earth. Feel the healing energies of Wicca driving through you as you breathe, pulled up as you breathe in and pushed down as you breathe out. This is the process of becoming connected to the world and allowing your abilities to travel over a greater distance.

Once you can feel the powers flowing through you, it is time to direct your energy. Take your hands from your legs and hold them above the crystal. Continue to breathe deeply, moving the energies that you have just found into the crystal and driving them towards the intended patient. The crystal is able to focus the energy and direct across great distances. On occasion, you may find that the crystal heats up and increases in temperature. Do not worry if this is the case. It can often be taken as a good sign, though it is not essential.

As you continue to direct the energy, discover the light of the candles as it is laid out before you. Notice the protective ring that they are able to form and focus this energy again through the crystal. The light that is created by these candles is a healing one, one that you are stretching across a great distance.

Finally, imagine the patient as you wish them to be. Imagine them healthy and well, emboldened by the power of Wicca which you have sent a great distance. If you know they are using medicine, then imagine that the drugs are even more effective and that the positive energies that are sent are coating them in a warm glow.

Once this is done. Place your hands back on your thighs and resume a regular breathing pattern. With the incense still burning, extinguish the candles and remove all of the items.

The energy which you have sent is complete, but allow the positive emotions to mix with the smell of the incense as it heals the patient.

Chapter 14 Divination spells

The final set of spells that we will lay out in this beginners' guide will deal with something a little more abstract. While many people are aware of Wicca and how it can influence the present, few are aware of the powerful divination abilities that it can provide. Rather than allowing you to see the future exactly as it will be, the following spells will allow you to feel the energies and spirits as they move towards the future. Those who practice more and more at these arts will be able to gain a greater understanding of the shape of the world to come.

The construction of a scrying mirror

The first step towards being able to practice the art of divination is to ensure that you have the correct tools available. For the most powerful witches, the tools are almost incidental, and the future can be seen in anything from tea leaves to dropped sticks. However, building up this level of ability is incredibly hard work, so most people begin with something a little simpler.

A scrying mirror is something which you can make at home. It can help you to look towards the future for a better understanding of how to approach the upcoming world. While you will be unlikely to view lottery results, it can help you discern the swell of energies which surround the future. To construct a scrying mirror for yourself, you will need:

- A mirror or an equally shiny object which will provide you with a reflective surface
- Mugwort infusion (created by placing mugwort in a sealed jar with boiling water and left to stew for days)

Because the mugwort infusion can be left to stew for so long, it can be preferable to plan this spell well in advance to be sure that you have everything available. If you are worried about the process of creating the infusion, we added a simple mugwort infusion recipe in the appendix at the end of the book. Once the infusion is ready, strain the leaves and pour away the water and we will begin.

The important part of this process is known as consecrating your mirror. This involves the act of imbuing a standard household object with magical properties, and telling the correct energies where they must pass. If you choose, you can call upon a chosen deity to help assist you with this task, or you can depend upon the power of nature itself. As long as you feel an affinity with the power on which you call, your mirror should be functional.

Once you are ready to begin, fill a container with the infusion which you have created, and place the mirror flat on a table. Take a moment to center yourself, directing your thoughts and energies towards the mirror. When you are ready, take a handful of the infusion and begin to spread it across the surface of the mirror, using the substance to guide your hand across the shiny surface. Be sure that you cover every inch of the mirror. As you carry out the task, imagine the energies flowing through your hand. Picture the mirror awakening and discovering the power it not possesses.

With this powerful new tool, there are a number of spells which are available to you. For most witches, the more powerful spells are those that are the most complicated. However, for those beginners with a clear interest in divination, the mirror can be used to practice and refine the fortune telling arts.

At first – and this is true for almost every beginner – the mirror will seem a strange and foreign object. For each witch, however, the process of learning how to use your particular scrying mirror will be unique. To get started and to discover the way in which you will work with your mirror, hang it on a wall in a room that you pass through very often. A hallway is an excellent choice as you will likely pass the mirror on the way to leaving the house. As you walk past it on the way out, pause for five seconds in front of the mirror. Close your eyes and focus your energy. When you open them again, you should be able to notice the ways in which your image alters slightly in the reflection.

Note these changes and note the events that then happen in your life. Over the course of time, you will build up an understanding of the changes and the effects which they predict. As mentioned above, divination required much practice, but creating and using a scrying mirror in this fashion can lead to a bright future of powerful magic.

Candle spells

As well as using a scrying mirror, many people find that candles are able to provide them with a great insight into the world of divination. For Wicca practitioners, there is a great deal of power in the candle and almost all spells make use of them in some fashion. So, to extend this power into fortune telling might not seem so strange. To get started, you can begin practicing on a single candle of any color or type.

First, find a seat at a table in a quiet room. Place the candle in front of you, and settle into a relaxed and almost meditative state. With the candle unlit, you should begin to form a strong mental image of the future that you wish to tell in your mind. To begin, try to focus on large events and happenings. These events will be easier to predict and much easier to latch on to than when you have no idea what you are searching for. Once you have a distinct image, light the candle.

Just as the candle is able to bring light into a dark room, the light here is able to shine a brightness into the depths of the future. As the light increases, you should begin to see your future image in a clearer and more distinct manner. Feel the energy swelling around the room, and allow it to make itself clearer and clearer. For many people, the first attempts are only flickering, and the images become very clear for a very short amount of time before vanishing. This is fine. Perfecting this art will typically be a case of being able to hold these images for longer and longer, getting a better look at what they suggest.

But these images are not the only information which you will have. Upon lighting the candle, the color of the smoke can give you a vague indication of the future. In a manner not unlike the way in which cardinals elect the next pope, a black color of smoke will indicate the process of negative energy being removed from the image which you have in your mind. If the smoke is white, then it might be that there will be some kind of delay and/or a struggle to come.

Should the flame of the candle be weak, then the truthfulness of the prediction is better founded, while a strong candle can often mean the opposite. The direction of the smoke can also be an indicator, with smoke that moves away from you likely to suggest the hastened acknowledgement of your desire. In some cases, the very act of trying to look into the future can speed up the movement and the process of actualization, helping you to achieve your goals as they become clearer.

As with the scrying mirror, however, the true art is in perfecting your interpretations. The power of Wicca is often in the practitioner. Being able to discern the exact meaning of the images that play out before you are often the best way in which you can perfect your divination abilities.

Conclusion

Magical practices aim to engage the earthly senses on an intimate level to allow our conscious mind to utilize a sort of 'sixth sense.' This sixth sense then, in turn, allows us to engage with other realms and beings that aren't readily seen with only five senses. These beings and realms were the homes and dwellings of our ancestors as they saw no difference between conscious experience and the experiences of dream realms and astral planes.

These practices are key to unlocking the secrets of humanity and ushering in the rebuilding of our spiritual evolution. Without magic, there is no progression for humanity's mind, Technology and science alone cannot push us beyond the heavens.

As you progress on your journey, keep in mind the Wiccan philosophy that as long as you are not harming anyone then do what you like. This is reminiscent of Crowley's 'do what thou wilt', this has become an umbrella philosophy more almost every magical community. A real magician will not be concerned with petty arguments over lineage or purity of practice, they will not segregate or discriminate, no, and they are beyond the earthly confines of prejudice.

Magicians also will not intentionally harm others if they are innocent, there is no need for violence or forceful magic to get your way. Be creative and always walk a righteous path that is full of love, discipline and understanding. These are the true virtues of magic and the essence of truth. So, may it be.

Witchcraft Moon Spells

How to use the Lunar Phase for Spells, Wiccan and Crystal Magic, and Rituals. A starter kit for Witchcraft Practitioners using the Mysteries of Herbs and Crystals Magic.

Linda Candles

Book Description

The moon has been a source of inspiration to human kind, and it has always had a very impactful position in the lore of the world throughout a number of different cultures across the world and throughout our history. The moon, as well as the sun, have both served very important purposes to us, and have seemingly always had very strong connections to the gods and goddesses that we have revered throughout human history. Similarly, to the sun, the moon is often associated with a large number of gods throughout the world from a number of different cultures. It is most commonly associated with a lot of the concepts and ideas that humans are commonly concerned with or about.

Some of the most common and most significant of these associations are the spirit, soul, heart, fertility, passion, and love as well as death, the afterlife, and rebirth and a large number of different mysteries to humanity. Of course, the moon is still a very significant part of regular life even today, and is still present in modern belief systems like Wicca and other forms of paganism and modern witchcraft.

Many wiccans will typically gather during the full moon in order to perform certain rituals that honor the wiccan goddess during each of the different Sebat's. Of course, the sun and the moon are not the only bodies that possess their own energy.

The earth also acts as an independent source of energy, as well as receiving energy from the sun and the moon. However, it does still receive some energy from the moon and the sun, which allow for the creation and the ability to sustain the life on the earth.

The energy that is produced by the moon is often thought to be "magnetic", in a sense, due to its size and proximity to the earth causing its gravitational pull to have a very strong impact on the life that exists on the earth. This is often the origin of the "pull" that some people will feel toward the moon on a clear night.

Some people, if they are particularly sensitive to these kinds of forces, might even feel a literal tugging sensation within their bodies during the new or full moon, but most people will simply notice a slightly stronger kind of connection with the moon during these moments.

This book gives a comprehensive guide on the following:

- What is Wicca?
- World of Wicca
- The Energy of the Moon
- The Eight Phases of the Moon
- Moon magic of the lunar cycle
- What Do Wiccans Believes

- Life-Changing Moon Manifesting Visualization Strategy
- Simple Spells and Rituals... AND MORE!!!

Introduction

In the broadest sense, Wicca, also known as The Craft, is a term used to encompass most forms of modern Pagan Witchcraft. Many people don't know what it means to be Wiccan, or who a witch might be today. In the past, throughout history, witches have been persecuted for being agents of evil or even Devil worshippers. While Wiccans certainly aren't perfect, as are none of us, they are no more evil than any other group of people with the same spiritual views. For Wicca it is not the practice of satanic worship nor Devil worship, Wicca is, in essence, the exact opposite to this and has nothing to do with the Dark Arts, unlike these stereotyped folklores.

To many people's surprise Wiccans encompass a broad spectrum of people as well. A Wiccan could be a typical businessman, that performs rituals every week as a high priest in his coven, or that nice older lady who lives down the block, and always used to send you cookies when she heard you were feeling down (You had no idea she was giving you healing energies, too!). Wiccans are doctors, and handymen, housewives and rock stars. Wicca is a way of life that many people share and a community of giving and acceptance worldwide. Wiccans are those who share and practice these beliefs and ideals. Yet the religion has no recognition of hierarchy, leadership or sectarianism. The beauty of Wicca as a belief system is that it is not limited to one religion or one ideal, yet open to all systems of beliefs as an adaptation to your way of living, to enhance your current belief system. In a narrower definition, Wicca is a religion developed and descended from British Traditional Wicca (BTW), or Witchcraft. Its core practices and rituals have come together over time throughout history. Yet it was not until the early 19th Century that this world was bought to the public attention after centuries of being stigmatized.

Many people refer to Gerald Gardener, also known as Scare, to be the father of Wicca. Due to his original development and culmination of these ancient practices throughout the 1940s and 1950s that Gardner and later with collaboration by Doreen Valiente, into what is known today as Wicca. These two spiritual pioneers outlined and developed what would later come to be known as part of today's British Traditional Wicca, drawing on a wide, and sometimes highly disputed set of ancient Pagan and Hermetic belief systems. This included but never limited to tapping into Freemasonry, Druidism, Shamanic work, modern science and medicine, calling upon works of the likes of Aleister Crowley. Other spiritual leaders in the Wiccan and Pagan community would leave their indelible marks on the rich, varied and sometimes misunderstood spiritual faith called Wicca. From fierce opposition in the form of scathing British scorn to the New

Age boom of Neo-Pagan and Wiccan theologies of the 1960s counterculture in the U.S.A. Two recent poles into American Religious Identification identify Wicca as one the fastest growing, evolving and ever-changing spiritual choice for millions of people.

The term Wicca itself is often disputed, yet has the roots to Anglo-Saxon language, meaning "wise one" this later was adopted in the Old English language to form term "witch," the term that many people have known practitioners of Wicca by for the last centuries. This original term was readopted due to the exploration into the ways of old and as a memoir back to the roots of Wicca's as a polytheistic belief system, as the word which was chosen by the Old British English and given a reputation for the Dark Arts throughout the Early Christian Era. Today, those who call themselves Wiccan are practitioners of a widely varied and diverse tradition, based in British Traditional Wicca, but encompassing many different offshoots and beliefs.

Chapter 1 What is Wicca?

Wicca is an active 20th century cult in contemporary witchcraft that helps its practitioners develop a deeper connection with Nature and Mother Earth. Through its teachings, the religion of Wicca promotes awareness, love and respect for the Sun and the sunlight, Moon, rivers, winds, rain and mountains, the animal kingdom, flowers and trees, the soil beneath our feet, the colorful autumn and the winter snow.

Wicca teaches us that everything that surrounds us is made of energy, and it embraces the principle of duality in all creation. This entails the existence of a God and Goddess, the masculine and feminine energy, the positive and negative. The whole Universe is made of such energy and Nature itself is a beautiful manifestation of the duality principle as we, human beings, hold the spark of duality within us.

In Wicca, Gods and Goddesses are within us and with us. Portrayed as much more mild and nurturing entities, they are not vengeful towards their children, they do not hold grudges and punish and do not create Heaven and Hell. Instead, they are ever loving, understanding and promote love and equality.

Wicca teaches us to accept full responsibility for our actions and does not support behavior and claims of an external entity such a Devil manipulating us into doing something bad.

This is where the teaching of Karma comes in and the idea that what you put out in the world comes back to you in the form of energy, people, and circumstances. Wiccans do not believe in Satan or any other representation of Evil. Such concepts are usually part of Christian teachings. Also, there is no claim of any exclusivity in terms of it being the only path to knowledge, peace, wisdom and divinity. Instead, the teachings of Wicca encourage the individual to seek out and choose his or her own path in life. This philosophy is based on the belief that Nature is sacred and that Life deserves respect regardless of the form through which it is manifested.

Wiccan Spells

Wiccan spells are frequently portrayed into two noteworthy sorts, "White magic" being related with high and considerate points and "Dark Magic" regularly connected with abhorrence deeds and evil love.

Numerous advanced Wiccans have stopped utilizing this duality, contending that the shading dark is simply one more shading that has been performed by Hollywood, and that the shading itself ought not to have any relationship with sinister ceremony or hatred by any stretch of the imagination.

Wiccans accept that magic spell casting is a fundamental law of nature. A law that we still can't seem to get it. Different devotees of the Wicca Religion don't profess to know how their magic works by any stretch of the imagination, and it is sufficient that it does work and that they have seen it work for themselves.

Most Wiccans characterize Wiccan spells or Wiccan Magic as "the Art of making changes happen in consistence with one's very own will." The term Wiccan essentially alludes to any individual who practices the Wiccan Religion.

A Wiccan spell is training or ritualized occasion which prompts quantifiable changes in the physical or enthusiastic circle as per the aims of at least one Wiccans who are casting the spell.

Wiccan magic spells ordinarily rehearsed incorporate love spells, mending spells, ripeness spells just as spells to help evacuate any terrible impacts.

The Wiccan Sacred Circle

Wiccans regularly cast spells during ceremonial practices within a develop called "the Sacred Circle," trying to realize changes to their reality.

A Sacred Circle is a circle or circle of room stamped blessed by Wiccans to either contain vitality and structure a sacred space or to shape a hindrance of security. The Sacred Circle can sometimes be both.

Sacred Circles are made by making a ring from salt or chalk. A few Wiccans will even scratch a line in the earth, and now and again it can essentially be envisioned by a Wiccan Witch to deliver similar outcomes. Comparative round develops show up in some Eastern religions.

Wiccan spells, in most of the occasions, are cast to help emerge an altruistic outcome. The fact of the matter is most of the magic spells cast by Wiccans (just as numerous different adherents and supporters of the "Old Religions") are cast for good and not malicious.

The Law of Threefold Return

This is exhibited by the Wiccan Rede, which essentially expresses "it hurt none, do what ye will." Many Wiccans likewise have faith in another component of Wiccan ethical quality which is "The Law of Threefold Return."

This law holds that paying little mind to what sort of Wiccan spell is cast, be it big-hearted or pernicious, the activities of the spell will return to the practitioner with triple the power or power.

This belief is fundamentally the same as the eastern way of thinking of Karma, first embraced in quite a while and later showing up in different structures in the Buddhist, Jain, Sikh and Hindu methods of reasoning. This is one motivation behind why Wicca is consistently alluded to as the yoga of the west.

Yoga as a whole is one of the six schools of Hindu way of thinking. Yoga is about control and preparing working together to enable the awareness to arrive at a condition of impeccable profound knowledge and serenity. Numerous advanced Wiccans will see this announcement as a reasonable meaning of their belief systems too.

Wiccan Spells come in numerous sorts and varieties since you practice your spell casting with a decent and kind mental demeanor, you will discover like huge numbers of that the old nature religions, for example, Wicca can be fulfilling and as satisfying the same number of progressively eastern and western belief systems.

Instructions to Create Your Wiccan Spells

Digging Into Witchcraft

If you discover spells that you have turned out to be fairly enamored with, however, you would feel significantly more grounded about them if you could "change" a couple of things, you can utilize spells offered in books or on the web. As you adjust spells to suit your inclinations, there are a few things you'll have to consider. Above all else, recollect that if you are adapting spells from different works, your adjustments are for your utilization as it were. A ton of agnostic journalists offer spells for adjustment; however, you certainly would prefer not to encroach on the copyright of writers or online scholars by sharing your adjusted works on the web or off, particularly without the consent from the first writers of the adjusted work.

Before you start composing or adapting spells by any means, ensure you consider what it is that you truly need; "watch what you wish for" is inferred here. Ensure you are clear about what you need, yet why you need it, and how you anticipate that your wants should manifest. You ought to likewise give full thought to any potential outcomes of your magickal workings; sometimes when you are working magick, you can wind up with the result that gives you decisively what you requested, yet not how you anticipated. This is why specificity is so essential to work.

Regardless of whether you are adapting spells you have turned out to be partial to or composing your spells without any preparation, you'll have to keep your aim in the back of your psyche. Each word in the spell needs to line up with your goal and the desired outcome. To that end, how specific you are with your spells will characterize the achievement of your spell casting tries. To loan to the specificity in your compositions, you can consummate the wording and timing of the work, and you can utilize magickal correspondences.

Timing - Some practitioners time a spell is working during a specific moon stage. For example, you can time spells during the waxing, full, or melting away moon stage. The waxing moon is related with beginnings and the winding down the moon with endings, while the full moon is related with all magickal workings. Along these lines, if you are directing a spell where you need a circumstance to end, you can time your work for when the winding down moon shows up, and if you are searching for another beginning in a circumstance, the waxing moon is the best time to play out your work. A few practitioners likewise time their work dependent on days of the week, the season, the planetary hours, or mysterious correspondences.

Rhymes - Not all spells rhyme, yet you may find that you are undeniably progressively open to working with rhyme. You'll see it simpler to recall, and when utilizing rhyme, you make a mood with your words when expressed so anyone might hear. When you compose your very own spells, you ought to invest some energy retaining what you've composed. Along these lines, you can give your complete consideration to what words you are expressing as opposed to understanding them from a bit of paper.

Perception - Your spell ought to contain exact wording that won't just help you verbally express your wants, yet you'll additionally need wording that triggers your representation capacities. The more seriously you can picture your desired manifestation, the more noteworthy the probability you will accomplish the outcome you look for. Indeed, before working a spell, it's a smart thought investing some energy picturing your desired outcome. Similarly, as with your spell's wording, when imagining, you should be as specific as could be allowed, seeing your desired outcome in each conceivable detail.

Inspiration - Finally, if you're a Witch rehearsing the Wiccan religion, you'll need to ensure that your spell's wording and expected outcome is lined up with the Wiccan Rede of, "hurt none, do what ye will." As a Wiccan practitioner, you ought to be worried about the Threefold Law of Return and the potential kickback that goes with the demonstration of conveying negative energies. Ensure your spell workings are sure with the goal that what returns to you in the method for manifestation is similarly positive.

How to become a wiccan

1. Peruse

Before you even consider changing over to Wicca, or before you settle on any concluded choices or statements, you ought to invest some energy contemplating. Sorry to learn this— however if you don't care for perusing or considering, you're most likely not going to like Wicca without question; or possibly you're not going to get much of anywhere. Wicca is a non-dogmatic religion; as opposed to disclosing to you what to accept, it tosses the ball in your court and guides you to think fundamentally. This requires information.

One book isn't sufficient, yet five or ten books is a decent start. It's by and large prescribed you read and study—effectively—

for in any event a year and a day before settling on any choices about whether to be Wiccan or not.

Step 2: Think

When you genuinely start finding out about Wicca, it's beliefs, it's precepts, and so forth., it's time to think about whether your beliefs are a match. Are your own beliefs something that can fall inside a Wiccan system?

Wicca is certainly not a dogmatic religion, and this is valid; so, anybody coming into it searching for a book of a sacred text or a rundown of charges is moving toward it from an inappropriate edge. In any case, Wicca is additionally not, as some more unfortunate sources have generally been putting it, "anything you need it to be." The issue with saying Wicca is anything is that you're saying it's nothing. There are a few things that don't fit very well under the definition.

For instance, if you don't have faith in any Gods, and you're simply hoping to practice enchantment, at that point why are you joining a religion in which the real rituals, celebrations, customs, and so on are focused on Pagan Gods and Goddesses? You could feel free to examine Witchcraft without getting to be Wiccan by any means. Or on the other hand, if you put stock in Jesus with your entire existence as a hero, why would you like to worship him inside a religion that instructs there is not something to be spared from?

The excellence of Wicca is that there are no commands—there are no 'acknowledge this or clear out' ways of thinking. In any case, in being a piece of an experiential religion, you are tolerating obligation to utilize rationale and reason—which means genuinely considering if your beliefs fit inside Wicca, or that if maybe a couple of things that draws in you to Wicca can be found in another religion that is more in accordance with your beliefs.

Step 3: Pray

When you come to the heart of the matter at which you realize you need to adore as a Wiccan, it's time to begin reversing. Start going to your Gods. Acquaint yourself and ask them to uncover themselves to you — request direction, for clarification, for comprehension.

Start ruminating—for as is commonly said, if supplication is conversing with your God, reflection is tuning in. An everyday reflection system can be gainful for wellbeing and health purposes, yet spiritual advancement.

Step 4: Observe

Start monitoring life from a Wiccan viewpoint. Watch the cycles of the seasons and the cycles of the moon. Start recognizing them in little ways. Consider Wiccan precepts and morals when you're looked with decisions. Think about your life, and territories in which exercises can be gained from Wicca.

Watch your general surroundings; the transaction between every living thing. Begin to see the cycles of the seasons, of the moon, of life. You may wish to get into an increasingly ordinary everyday practice with your reflections and supplications or start some extremely straightforward, casual rituals to observe Esbats and Sabbats.

Now, perusing and learning shouldn't stop, yet it's critical to begin some utilization of those standards. That is how you start living Wicca.

Step 5: Build

A misstep many individuals make right off the bat is hurrying out to gather tools—however, Wicca isn't a scrounger chase. In any case, now, when you've started to practice, you might need to begin moving towards progressively formal practice. You may wish to begin gathering special raised area tools— you don't need to get them at the same time. It's a smart thought to examine a tool and its motivation, at that point, search for it, begin to utilize it, doing this each in turn.

Many books will guide you to get various things; however, remember that you won't need each tool that each book refers to. This is why it's critical to comprehend a tool's capacity before you even stress over getting it—it might end up being something you needn't bother with.

It's likewise time to start fabricating your ritual. That is, building an increasingly organized way to deal with your ritual. That doesn't mean you need to design every single detail out; however, by its very definition, a ritual is a rehashed demonstration. The redundancy encourages you to arrive at ritual cognizance. It helps you to sidestep the condition of awareness where you're effectively thinking into that state in which you go into 'autopilot' with the goal that you can open yourself to the different energies you're attempting to raise.

Start pondering a standard opening and shutting, summons, throwing a circle. Once more, it's not something you need to do across the board night. However, every couple of months consider and include another component.

Step 6: Magic

Enchantment isn't the focal point of Wicca. However, it's positively a noteworthy segment. In the end, you're going to need to join some into your practice. Somebody intrigued by simply learning enchantment doesn't need to be Wiccan and ought to go directly to learning The Craft; however, if Wicca as a religion is the thing that premiums you, invest the energy acclimating yourself with the religion first. When you come to the heart of the matter at which you're gathering tools and holding standard rituals, it's a decent time to begin rehearsing this intriguing and charming component. Begin including some minor mysterious functions in your hover, just as beginning examinations in expressions of the human experience.

Step 7: Network

Sooner or later, it's beneficial for you to get out in the Pagan people group on the loose. There is no need to hold up until the conclusion to do this, yet if you haven't, yet, you should attempt now.

Meet with different Wiccans, go to classes or open rituals or drumming circles. Doing this can open you to numerous new thoughts, help you discover individuals to converse with that you can identify with, you may even discover a coven that you'd like to join if this is your definitive objective. Religions are close to home adventures, but on the other hand, they're intended to be experienced publicly somewhat.

This rundown is in no way, forms or shapes the best way to approach getting to be Wiccan, and however, if you're uncertain of where to begin or where to go, it's a decent progression that will get you on your way.

Wiccan rituals

Regardless of whether the event is a Sabbat, an Esbat, or an achievement, for example, a handfasting (wedding), a commencement, or a part of the arrangement, covens and circle individuals will assemble to love together, respect the Goddess and God, and commend the marvels to be found in the progressing cycles of life. While most Wiccan rituals are apprehended in private, a few covens will every so often hold theirs out in the open, with the goal that all who wish to watch can come and get familiar with the Craft. Many Wiccan circles do likewise, and may even welcome people in general to take part.

Solo rituals are no less significant, and single Wiccans realize that as they worship at each point along the Wheel of the Year, they include their light and power to the group supernatural energy on these exceptional events.

RUDIMENTS OF WICCAN RITUALS

Beautiful, baffling, rich, and encouraging, Wiccan rituals can take a wide range of structures, with no two occasions being similar. Some might be exceptionally organized and expound. This is frequently the situation with coven rituals, and however since most covens keep the subtleties of their rituals mystery, known uniquely to started individuals, it's difficult to depict them with much precision. Different rituals, especially those practiced by solitary and diverse Wiccans, might be genuinely basic by correlation, and may even be made up on the spot.

The substance of some random Wiccan ritual will rely upon the event. For instance, Esbats, or Full Moon festivities, are focused exclusively on the Goddess, while Sabbats respect the co-inventive connection between the Goddess and the God. In spite of all the potential varieties, be that as it may, there are a couple of essential elements that will, in general, be incorporated into what we may call a "common" ritual.

To begin with, there is a purification, both of the celebrant(s) and where the ritual is held. This can occur as a ritual shower, or potentially a smearing service to expel any unwanted energies from the ritual space, regardless of whether it's an outside territory or inside the home. Smearing includes the consuming of sacred herbs, for example, sage, rosemary, as well as lavender.

Setting up the altar comes straightaway. A few Wiccans can keep an altar forever set up in their homes, however even for this situation, and it will probably be enhanced differently relying upon the event, for example, acquiring fall foliage for Mabon (the Autumn Equinox) or Samhain (otherwise called Halloween.) The altar is organized with the different Wiccan tools, images, and contributions, spread out as indicated by any of various traditions.

Next comes the throwing of the circle, a demonstration that makes a limit between the sacred space and the common, commonplace world. The altar is commonly at the focal point of the circle, with a lot of space for all required to work openly inside the circle, with no inadvertent venturing outside of the energetic limit. The circle might be set apart with sea salt, a long line, a few stones, herbs, or candles. There are numerous techniques for circle-throwing, which you can peruse progressively about here.

When the circle is thrown, the summons start. The order here can shift, however regularly the God and Goddess are welcome to join the ritual, and after that, the four Elements— Earth, Air, Fire, and Water—are summoned, as these are the crude materials that make up all of the presence. (In numerous traditions, a fifth Element—Akasha, or Spirit—is additionally brought in.) In different traditions, this progression is known as Calling the Quarters, and the four bearings (North, East, South, and West) are tended to, either rather than or notwithstanding the Elements.

When these means have occurred, the core of the ritual starts. To begin with, the aim of the event is expressed—regardless of whether it's to commend a Sabbat or an Esbat, or maybe to request of the God and Goddess for the benefit of somebody who needs mending or some other sort of help. (Enchanted spellwork can to sure be the focus of a ritual. However, numerous Wiccans will do this independently from Sabbat festivities, to maintain the focus on the Goddess and God during Sabbats.)

After the goal is expressed, the principle body of the ritual may comprise of different exercises. The point of convergence might be the presentation of a ritual show, for example, reenacting scenes from antiquated fantasies or ballads—or other ritualistic material, contingent upon the tradition of Wicca the gathering is following. Solitary Wiccans may likewise peruse from antiquated otherworldly messages, or make their very own verse for the event. Reciting, singing, moving and additionally other ritual motions might be a piece of the procedures, as might just thinking about casually the gifts of the season. Petitions may be offered, regardless of whether they are personal or for the benefit of others. It's basic in certain traditions to utilize ritual space to expect to help a whole network or even all of humanity.

In numerous traditions, a service known as "cakes and beer" (or "cakes and wine") is a significant piece of Wiccan rituals. Sustenance and drink are offered and emblematically imparted to the God and Goddess, ordinarily toward the part of the arrangement of the ritual (albeit a few traditions start with it). This function associates the spiritual plane with the Earth plane, and grounds and focus the members before shutting the ritual procedures. When it's an ideal opportunity to part of the arrangement, Elements and the Goddess and God are officially expressed gratitude toward and discharged, and the circle is shut.

Once more, this is only an essential format that a Wiccan ritual would commonly pursue. If you join a setup coven or circle, the gathering will in all probability have its very own rendition of what's been depicted above, with numerous potential varieties. If you're a solitary specialist, you can research a specific tradition to pursue, or you can make your very own interesting Wiccan rituals. For whatever length of time that your aim is earnest and you are focused on your activities, there's no real way to get it "wrong"!

Pretty much every religion joins sacred items into its recognition and practice. Regardless of whether its uncommon vestments worn by religious officiants, statues of gods respected at sanctuaries, candles, talismans, chalices or other emblematic items, individuals have been making and using physical artifacts—or "tools"— to make and keep up spiritual energy and focus in their ritual practices.

Wicca includes the utilization of a few tools, every one of which has its representative significance, specific uses, and specific situation on the Wiccan altar during a ritual.

A "HANDS-ON" PHILOSOPHY

Wiccan ritual tools are utilized to focus and direct spiritual (or "mystic") energy for the reasons for interfacing legitimately with the perfect. There's an unobtrusive yet significant qualification, nonetheless, between this practice and the utilization of emblematic items in different religions. Wiccans perceive that they share in the co-innovative powers of nature as typified by the Goddess and God, instead of being subject to the desire of a higher power.

This way, the tools of Wiccan ritual are both emblematic and down to earth, as each article and each activity performed inside the circle of sacred energy is intentionally expected to tackle and direct this co-imaginative power. Tools are utilized to summon and invite divinities and the energies of the Elements, to perform mystical work, and to secure against undesirable energetic impacts, among different capacities. Notwithstanding, it's critical to perceive that the tools don't have supernatural powers all by themselves—they function as courses of the personal power of the Wiccan who uses them.

"THE LIST" OF WICCAN TOOLS

The precise arrangement of ritual tools viewed as at the center of Wiccan practice will change contingent upon the tradition. A few covens and solitaries watch exceptionally expand rituals utilizing an assorted cluster of articles, while others keep things generally basic, utilizing a few tools for various ritual capacities. That being stated, the most regularly referred to tools utilized in an essential ritual is the chalice (or cup), the wand, the pentacle, the athame (or ritual knife, articulated "a-that-may"), the censer (for incense), and at least one candles.

Other as often as possible referenced tools—which, once more, might be viewed as basic tools relying upon tradition—are the broom, the cauldron, the ringer, the sword, the staff, and the ritual scourge. Besides, there are various items that add to ritual however are not considered "tools" all by themselves, for example, pictures of the God and Goddess, a boline (an exceptional knife utilized for cutting and cutting), a plate for ritual nourishment and additionally different contributions, precious stones and herbs, altar materials and beautifications, and so on.

It's not in the slightest degree essential to have these things in your own to begin rehearsing Wicca. It's by and large prescribed to start little, get tools each or two in turn, and steadily construct your ritual practice as you go.

STARTING POINTS OF RITUAL PRACTICE

To individuals new to Wicca, these tools can appear to be, to some degree, irregular and discretionary. Why are things like blades, cups, ringers, and pentacles regarded fundamental for communing with soul energy? There are numerous potential responses to this inquiry, at the end of the day it requires some investment, study, and tolerance all together for the tools of ritual to make genuine "sense" to an expert. This is a major piece of the purpose behind the custom of reading for a year and a day before committing oneself to the practice of Wicca. What's more, it realizes as much as you can about the historical backdrop of Wicca's improvement, just as the numerous spiritual traditions it draws from, some of which go back to the relic.

Chapter 2 World of Wicca

What many people all around the world don't understand is that Wicca is an actual religion, also known as 'Benevolent Witchcraft', 'The Old Religion', and 'The Craft'. This ancient craft is a part of our modern paganism or is also known as nature spirituality.

Paganism is a name for those who follow a religion or practice which is not Christianity, Judaism, Buddhism, or Hinduism. The Wiccan religion is a part of Paganism along with Pantheists, Heathens, Goddess Spirituality folk, Ecofeminist, Unitarian Universalist Pagans, Animists, Druids, ChristoPagans, and any other Nature related spirituality practices.

But within those religions, there are a variety of groups, all with different purpose, practices, size, orientation, structure, and symbology. There are many different types of practices within the Wiccan religion, such as Shamanic, Alexandrian, British Traditionalist, Gardnerian, Faerie, Hereditary or Family tradition, Celtic, Circle Crat, Dianic, Eclectic Craft, and many other paths and traditions.

Certain of those groups have other different specific practices and groups. Some of the Wiccan religion groups are initiatory, while there are others who are not. Many of those initiatory practices vary from different traditions; several of those groups have initiations by spiritual helpers, teachers, groups, and deities within dreams, visions, and vigils quests.

There are many differences between a variety of groups and religions, but they all respect and love Nature. Many seek to live in peace and harmony with the world and the ecosystem around them. Many practitioners are able to communicate and become friends with many plants, animals, and spirits that occupy the Earth along with us. They even honor the natural cycles of nature, such as the new moon and the full moon. Many love to perform rituals during these times, harnessing the energy of the element of earth. Those who follow the Wiccan religion are referred to as 'witches'.

In this Wiccan religion and other Paganism religions, it's a belief that every human, stream, animal, rock, tree, and other forms of nature possess a Divine Spirit located within. This is why in many traditions, apart from Paganism, they have a monotheistic dimension in which there is only one Divine God that they worship. In Paganism and some other traditions, they have a polytheistic dimension in which there are a variety of Divine forms including Gods, Goddesses, and many other spiritual forces. Nature and the universe play a big role in the way the Wiccan religion is shaped.

Chapter 3 The Energy of the Moon

The energy of the moon and the sun have shaped our development throughout our history, as well. Humans, as well as all other forms of life on earth, all maintain a strong connection to the energies of our celestial bodies, especially with the moon, which is the origin of a lot of the sensations and feelings that we will often refer to as our "intuition", which is why many people will consider women to be more naturally intuitive than men; they have a much stronger connection to the feminine energies that the moon emits, resulting in their higher level of intuitive talent compared to men.

This sensitivity to the energies of the sun and the moon are often referred to as our "sixth sense", and is arguably one of the most significant tools that we have access to when practicing any form of magic but this applies specially to moon magic.

When we are practicing moon magic, one of the most common ways to begin is to "appeal" to the moon and form a connection to it for the duration of the spell, but this connection that is formed is somewhat false; what is really happening is that the connection that we already possess with the moon is strengthened as we open ourselves up to the moon's energy and allow the pathway formed by this energy to be increased in size.

When this is done in the presence of the moon, and especially during the periods of the full moon and the new moon, when its power is strongest, this connection will allow us to greatly strengthen the spells and other kinds of magical work that we perform.

It is important to understand, however, that the different phases of the moon will produce slightly different energies that will be useful for different kinds of purposes or for different kinds of spells.

Each of the different phases of the moon carries a different kind of energy, which can be useful for different kinds of magic, and to accomplish different kinds of goals.

Our relationship with the moon about the magic that we perform with the energy that it provides us with seems to wax and wane with the different phases of the moon itself.

As the moon is waxing, its energy moves toward its peak and it will be able to much more effectively serve magic that is meant to increase potential or energy, while the magic that is performed during the later half of the lunar cycle is best used for magic that is meant to decrease the strength of energies or potential, such as banishing or cleansing unwanted energies.

The middle point during the cycle of the moon is commonly referred to as the harvest, and is the time to celebrate for the accomplishments that have been made and the spoils that have been reaped from the first part of the lunar cycle, similarly to the harvest that it is named for.

The second half of the lunar cycle is then dedicated to cleaning up after the fact and releasing the energies and the things that are not needed any more.

During the new moon, new intentions are set for the new cycle which will be manifested in the same way and ultimately dismissed as we move on to the cycle after that.

The lunar cycle ultimately represents a progression through time following a healthy course of events that allow for the creation of new things that will eventually be removed in order to allow more new things to be made in an endless cycle of renewal.

There are also a few basic tips for how to further empower the magical work that you perform at different points throughout the different stages of the cycle of the moon. For example, the first stage of the lunar cycle is the new moon. During the new moon, the energy that we receive from the moon will be particularly well suited for setting intentions for the rest of the month or for thinking about the things that you might want to build. Starting new tasks or projects will be much more effective during this phase of the moon's cycle, and any magical work that you perform involving the attraction of specific energies will be very effective during this period.

The second phase, when the moon will be rising to its highest point when it is full, is referred to as the waxing moon. This is the best phase of the lunar cycle for utilizing the energies that we receive from the moon in order to help us in moving forward toward the goals that we have set. This is the next logical step after starting up new projects, to move forward and to take action in order to begin to accomplish those goals.

The energy that you receive during this phase will be especially helpful for allowing us to reach the goals that we may have set, and can be very effective if it is applied to spell work that is related to the increase of various different kinds of energies. Some common examples are strengthening or building bonds between or among different people, or improving the physical or mental health.

The stage opposite to the waxing moon is the waning moon. This phase comes immediately after the full moon and before the new moon. The energy that you will receive during the full moon will be best for purposes opposite to the energy of the waxing moon.

The spellwork that you perform with the energy of the waning moon will be best used for things like releasing energies in order to overcome obstacles in your path or for cleansing yourself of negative energies.

The phase of the lunar cycle that is often considered the one that contains the most powerful energy is the full moon. Many people will believe the full moon to be the most magically significant day of the lunar cycle, and will take the opportunity to use the energy of the full moon for spells that are especially important. This is the reason for legends of werewolves or vampires, or a number of other kinds of supernatural or magical beings and events occurring on the night of the full moon.

This is when the moon and its power are at their highest points, and will be much more universally effective than during the other phases of the moon's cycle.

The moon's cycles start with the new moon. At this time the moon and sun are perfectly aligned but the sun's reflection faces away from Earth and this is why we can't see her glowing.

During this time the moon will rise and set during the day and it is sometimes impossible to see her without using a telescope. New beginnings and the new moon are pretty much the same things.

During these times, you need to focus on the things you want to manifest in your life such as new intentions and projects.

Harnessing the New Moon's Energy. Being able to visualize is the main key here. Where your thoughts go, your energy will flow. You have to bring awareness to the energy you are working with and the things you want to bring to life. If you have conscious thoughts and can direct your intentions and energy, everything you want in life is possible.

Create a Vision Board. You have to make your desires tangible things. Things that you can touch, look at and bring to life.

This can be done with poster board, magazine clippings, and glue or you can go digital and make a board on Pinterest. Your goal is to put all your intentions in one place.

When you have finished the board, look at each item and imagine the steps you need to take to make it happen. Will this take a lot of work? Will you need to ask for help from others? What do you need to do to get things moving?

Find some inspiration by defining the process for every intention. Inspiration will build momentum and momentum brings results.

Make a Sigil and Burn It. Sigils are a great way to get creative while pouring your intentions, energy, and love into your work.

The first thing you do is find some pieces of paper and start writing out statements that you want to manifest during the moon's cycle.

After you have your statement, take it just as it is stated and think about all the outcomes that might be possible. It might say: "I would like to live in abundance."

That's fine and dandy but the abundance of what? Do you want an abundance of negativity? Would you like to have an abundance of weight? You have to get specific. If you were to say: "I want to live a healthy, happy life full of abundant love".

This is a lot clearer, isn't it? Once you send these out into the Universe there can't be any confusion about what you are setting fire to. Try to keep away from using alternate definition if at all possible. Now that you have your intention, it is time to write it again without any spaces and get rid of all the vowels and any letters that repeat. It would look something like:

"wntlvhypfbd"

This is a bit hard to read, isn't it? Now from this point, you begin to combine the words to make a symbol. Place the legs and arms in places they shouldn't be and let your creative juices flow. There aren't any wrong symbols. By the time you are through, it should feel right. If it doesn't, start over and work it until it does feel right.

Once you have it, it is something that has taken your love, intention, attention, and time. You have worked both sides of the brain to make this wish. Within the first three days of the moon's cycle, so you can harness the moon's energy, you need to burn it to release your power and intentions out into the Universe to start manifesting.

Momentum and the Waxing Moon. There are three phases of the waxing moon and all of them have to do with getting yourself ready to achieve and receive your new intentions.

Waxing Gibbous Moon: During this time, you need to redefine your goals and get in tune with them. Use what has happened during the past few weeks to figure out what you need to do to refine your intentions. Things should be a lot clearer because you have taken steps and gotten insight on your goals and how they are coming along.

First Quarter Moon: This is the best time to take action. Figure out the steps you need to do to reach your goals. Don't get off course when an obstacle arises. You have to push forward during this time.

Waxing Crescent Moon: During this time, you need to imagine and plan your intentions. Send your desires, dreams, and hopes out into the world and focus on ways these things are going to affect your life.

Harvest Time. Things have already been set in motion from this and other new moons. This is the best time and it is waiting for you to cash in all your gifts. Look at what is sitting right in front of your face.

Have any opportunities presented themselves to you that you might have missed? Do you feel a force pushing you in new directions?

You have to be vigilant, aware, and open. You have to listen with your heart to be able to hear what the moon has to say. She has the power, wisdom, and words to transform your life.

Harnessing the Full Moon's Energy. The moon's energy is most powerful when she is full. Visualization is great during a new moon.

Charging yourself physically is great during the full moon. Get outside and greet the beautiful full moon with an open soul, mind, and heart.

This is the time for positive opportunities if you know how to use it right. It could increase your positive energy, or it could create havoc with your emotions.

Because the full moon brings a lot of energy, you have to make sure your mind is calm in order to receive all the positive effects. Remember that whatever is happening to your spirit, mind, or body is going to be amplified tremendously.

If you feel angry, you are going to feel even angrier. If you feel happy, you are going to feel even happier.

When the moon is full, the ocean will swell, and the emergency rooms will always have more patients. Her energy is extremely powerful so make sure you direct it along with positive intentions.

Loving energy and crazy energy will all be intensified. Just know that this is a great opportunity for you to grow spiritually and emotionally.

Here are some ways for you to use the full moon's energy to bring good things into your life:

Send out blessings to people who need it. Because the full moon's power is behind you, you can send the pink light of loving to strangers, colleagues, family, and friends along with forgiveness, and healing energy. You can also send peaceful energy out into the world that might be experiencing war, poverty, hardship, and strife. It will give them a lot of benefits and you have just created a huge load of karma. During a full moon is the best time to do acts of kindness and be of service to others.

Meditate. When you pray, you are speaking with your god. When you meditate, you are allowing these gods to talk to you. Bathe in the moon's glow and just breathe. Meditate as long as your body can take it and drink in all the connections, energy, and wisdom that is flying through the universe toward you. Because the full moon gives off so much energy, you need to create stillness, mindfulness, and calm. This can be done alone or in a sacred space.

You can also connect with other friends or a group. You should be able to find a spiritual center, yoga studio or online group that will come together to meditate during a full moon. This is extremely powerful when you meditate in a group. The ocean's tides are highest during this time and this means your tide will be high, too. You need to use this to get those messages; otherwise, they will just be falling on closed ears.

Visualize your dreams being manifested. During the full moon is a great time to work on your manifesting techniques. Take some time to imagine your goals and they write them down on paper. It is also a good time to look at your vision board to see if you need to make any changes.

Make sure your vision board is where you can see if every day. Take the time to focus on your dreams during the full moon to give them an extra boost.

Be positive. Everyone knows we need to think positively as often as possible during a full moon so you will have the wind at your back. Positive thoughts get multiplied and energized. Even if you just take five minutes after you get up and right before you go to bed to think about all the positive things you have in your life, you will be doing a great thing for your life. You could write out a gratitude list.

You could write the Universe a thank you note for everything you have received. Look at yourself in the mirror and tell yourself nice things. Talk a walk and see all the beauty around you. Visualize your positive thoughts have been sprinkled with the glitter of the full moon to make them grow larger and larger.

Don't get angry or argue. You have to stay calm during the full moon. You have to forgive others, breathe deeply during difficult moments, and let things go. If you can't let things go, you have to communicate them with others. Try to postpone talking about what has upset you until the full moon has been gone for two days. The things that happen during this time gets multiplied. It is like pouring fertilizer on your emotions. Keep your energy moving in an uplifting, happy direction whether you are in your car, work, home, and in all your daily interactions.

Family and Friends Bonfire. Have someone play the drums, be present, breathe, and dance around the flame's energy. I was told by an elder that the spirits will see you better by the light of a fire, so make sure you are lighting the way for your spirit guides to find you so they can give you their message. Make sure you are willing and ready to receive it.

Release and the Waning Moon. Just like the waxing moon, there will be three waning moons' during the month.

Everyone will help you move toward surrendering and releasing the Universe's plan along with your fate.

Waning Crescent: This is the last phase of the moon's cycle and it has the lowest vibrations. You might feel exhausted and drained, but this is completely normal during this phase. This phase wants you to recuperate and relax because you have cut ties with things that have been holding you back. While it is normal to feel tired, it is also important to surrender to any feelings you may have.

Feel them, heal them and move on. You are trying to manifest greatness and it will take some hard decisions and hard work.

Third Quarter: This is the best time for release. Are there things that are holding you back from reaching your ultimate goals? Is it a relationship? A job? A project that has been sucking your life out of you? Find all the things that are taking away your creativity and energy. Start getting rid of these things. If something isn't serving your greater purpose, now's the time to get it out of your life.

Waxing Gibbous: Now is the time for inner reflection and introspection. Review your goals by turning inward. Make sure you have the right intentions to pursue everything that is in your line of vision. Are the things you do for the correct reasons? Will the goals you have set serve the greater good in your life? Reflect on what your goals are and redefine them if you need to.

There isn't any reason why you have to wait until the start or end of a moon cycle to begin using her energy. You can begin anytime and any day you would like. Find the moon phase for your area and jump in with both feet.

Look at how the moon has already affected your life and use her energy to move you forward in the flow of the Universe.

Chapter 4 The Eight Phases of the Moon

"I see the moon and the moon sees me." Women have always had a profound connection with the moon. Women crave their mystic properties, guidance, and attention. We yearn for it, just like other people yearn for daylight.

The moon makes us feel powerful. We gain strength and energy from her presence. We just need to learn how to live during each phase of the moon.

The moon is thought of as female in astrology. She presides over our monthly cycles, emotions, and fertility. All females can be affected by her pull. It recedes and renews just like the tides.

We feel drawn between times of introspection and introversion and we have moments of extreme energy and passion.

History can't even deny the role that the moon can play on us. The word "lunatic" comes from many different languages that reference hysteria or madness. From the Latin word "lunaticus," that originally referenced to madness and epilepsy because they thought diseases were caused by the moon; and from the Old English "monseoc," "lunatic" actually translates to "moon-sick."

Pliny the Elder, the Roman historian and Aristotle, the Greek philosopher thought that since our brains are an organ that is "moist" that our minds could be influenced by the moon's pull just like the tides.

Ujjwal Chakraborty states in his paper, **Effects of Different Phases of the Lunar Month on Humans** that many studies have concluded there is an association between the lunar phases and human reproduction, patterns of physical activity, diseases, physical health, and mental health.

Elizabeth Palermo found a similarity between the words "month" and "moon" aren't a coincidence.

Every phase of the moon: last quarter, full, first quarter, and new; everyone happens one time every month. Speaking scientifically, these phases happen due to the distance between the moon and sun and how much light gets reflected onto the moon from the Earth.

It takes the moon about 29 and a half days to orbit the Earth and during this full orbit, we can see every phase of the moon. Every phase happens about 7.4 days apart.

There are very unique spiritual meaning and energies behinds every phase. Science is able to explain some of them. The others are where faith, experience, and belief have to take over.

Living their life according to the lunar phases have always had special meanings to women since we are physically and emotionally following these same phases. When the moon has to renew, withdraw, and recede every month, we have to, too.

We travel across various emotional states the exact same way the moon orbits the Earth. The more in tune we are to the phases and the way they affect us; we can learn to harness those energies instead of wasting our energy trying to fight them.

New Beginnings – New Moon

Spiritually: New moon is representative of a woman's menstrual cycle and throughout history, women lived away from other people during this time.

Don't think about the new moon as a fresh start but a time to retreat. During this time, you can start over and renew your strength. Clean slates, fresh starts, and new beginnings surround the new moon. You need to use this time to "reboot".

Imagine your "battery" getting recharged under the new moon's energy. Throw all your unwanted junk and thoughts away.

In order to do this, you have to unplug yourself and take some time alone. You might begin to feel introverted and anti-social. Watch for these feelings and just embrace them.

When the moon turns her dark side toward us, turn away from other people's draining energy and turn inward. Never feel bad if you have to cancel plans, you don't want to answer phone calls, or be around other people.

Turning off and tuning out is the best way to make it through a new moon.

Scientifically: The new moon begins when the moon and sun are both on the exact same side of the Earth. Since the sun isn't facing the moon, from our view on Earth, it looks as if the moon's dark side is facing us.

Setting Intentions – Waxing Crescent

Spiritually: This phase of the moon brings wishes, hopes, and intentions. Once you have recharged yourself under the new moon, your desires and intentions have been planted.

This is the time you need to develop your intentions, lay the groundwork for your next project, write checks to the Universe, and bury crystals.

Scientifically: When the moon begins to move closer to the sun it begins to get lighter. You will be able to see a crescent, less than half the moon will be lit until it begins to get bigger or waxes into the first quarter.

Action – First Quarter Moon

Spiritually: Since the first quarter moon happens one week after the new moon, this is the time that we begin to feel resistance from obstacles. If you planted intentions during the new moon, you will experience your first hurdles here. Actions, decisions, and challenges will all be faced during this time.

Your time of setting intentions and rest is finished and now you have to work harder. Get ready to have to make decisions quickly and don't lose your temper if things pop out of nowhere at you.

The easiest way to hand the moon is learning to be flexible. Keep your intention you set during the new moon on your mind the whole time. Make sure the decisions you make will bring the outcome to your intentions.

The best way to begin acting on them is to keep a journal. You need to physically write and act on your intentions. Create a daily list of things you need to do and mark them off as you finish them.

Scientifically: The moon will reach its first quarter one week after the new moon. We call this the first quarter because the moon is one-quarter of the way through the monthly phase.

Refine – Waxing Gibbous

Spiritually: Editing, refining, and adjustment surround the moon during this time. Things won't always work out the way we might have wanted to and this moon phase might help you see what you need to change directions on, give up on, or reevaluate.

If you would like to reap all the benefits of the full moon, you might need to sacrifice some things. You might need to change your course. Never resist the feelings of change during this phase.

Scientifically: The waxing moon is just one phase from turning into a full moon. This moon can be easily seen in the daytime since there is a huge portion that is lit up.

Harvest – Full Moon

Spiritually: Since the moon and sun are on opposite sides of the Earth, they are also in completely opposite zodiac signs, too. This can bring more tension because we are fighting to find a balance between these extremes.

Emotions will run high during this time. It is very important not to get extremely attached or emotional to anything during this time.

The first full moon during September is called the Harvest Moon.

This is the time that farmers will harvest their crops. Just like they are reaping the benefits of the seeds they planted earlier in the year, you need to be reaping all the benefits from your intentions that you set during the new moon.

You might see these benefits show up as results from all the hard work you've done. They might show up as new opportunities, too. Be sure that you are open and prepared to receive them.

Scientifically: A full moon will happen when the moon and sun are on opposite sides of the Earth. Since the sun is sitting directly across from the moon, the light is lighting it up completely. This makes the moon look full when you see it from the Earth.

Grateful – Waning Gibbous

Spiritually: Enthusiasm, sharing, and gratitude surround the moon during this phase. You should feel all the benefits of the hard work you've done in the past two weeks. Your "crops" are abundant, and you should see some, even if they are small, outcomes from your intentions and goals you have set.

Now is the time you will be feeling full of love. You want to give back to the people around you.

You might treat your partner to a night out on the town. You might buy your friend a present just because you saw something, and it reminded you of them.

You might find yourself spending more money this week than you normally do. Don't go overboard on your spending but don't feel bad about what you have spent on the people you love. Giving back is the main theme during this phase.

Scientifically: Once the full moon has passed, the moon begins to be less lit again. It wanes toward the last quarter moon and then back to another new moon.

Release – Last Quarter

Spiritually: Forgiveness, letting go, and release surround the moon during this phase. Just like the moon is slowly getting smaller, you need to be ready to get rid of stuff. During the month you might have been angered, broken, or hurt.

During this phase of the moon is when you can release all this anger and grudges. You have to purge yourself in order to receive the intentions you will be set during the next new moon.

A good practice during this phase is cleansing. Clean out your closets, look at friendships, and clean out your house. Look for anything that isn't serving you and toss it out.

Watch out for unnecessary physical and emotional clutter that you might have accumulated during the past phases and get rid of it. In order to get rid of all this unnecessary emotional baggage, do whatever physical activity that you enjoy.

Scientifically: This phase of the moon is the complete reverse of the first quarter as it makes its way to another new moon. After a full moon, the moon will wane and get smaller. It turns into another gibbous moon, and then into the last quarter.

Surrender – Waning Crescent

Spiritually: Recuperate, rest, and surrender. You might feel completely drained during this time. You have lived through a whole moon cycle and things have happened.

You might have let things go and received things. You might have willingly received or let things go or you might have fought some things. You need to prepare for a new moon and a new cycle and there isn't anything wrong with setting new intentions but not during this phase.

Right now, you need to surrender to the Universe and relax. Some things are always going to be out of your control and fate has to have its way.

Scientifically: The last bit of moon that is lit up is getting smaller and it is on the way to be a new moon.

Chapter 5 Moon magic of the lunar cycle from new moon to full moon and back

Since the primary stirrings of human progress, the Moon has assumed a significant job in the fantasies and practices of societies around the globe. For ages, it filled in as both a wellspring of light and a method for estimating time. Like its partner, the Sun, it has been connected with numerous divine beings and goddesses around the world. In both fantasy and magic, this heavenly body has been all around related with numerous focal worries of human presence, for example, love, enthusiasm, richness, secret, demise and resurrection, and the afterlife. Today, the Moon is as yet a fundamental nearness in Wicca and different types of current Witchcraft and Paganism. Generally, Wiccan covens meet for Full Moon customs to respect the Goddess on the Esbats, a practice received by solitaries also.

THE POWER OF THE MOON

Researchers realize that the Earth has its energy, which is free from the energy it gets from the Sun. The Moon additionally transmits energy that is unobtrusive yet particular. In contrast to the Sun's manly, projective energy, lunar energy is ladylike and open. This is the energy of the Goddess. This power has frequently been portrayed as attractive, which bodes well to any individual who has felt "pulled" somehow or another by the Moon. Some especially delicate individuals feel a physical pull in their bodies at the Full or New Moon, while others see an elevated feeling of attention to everything in their condition.

Lunar energy is customized for cooperating with the energy of possessing instinct, which is additionally female, responsive, and attractive. Otherwise called the intuition, this is the most urgent method of observation when it comes to magic. So, when we intentionally associate with the energy of the Moon, we are opening up a pathway, or channel, for that energy to help manifest wanted changes in lives. Furthermore, when we do this in cognizant agreement with the vivacious rhythms of the Moon's cycle, we can amplify the intensity of the magical work. This is because each stage of the lunar period offers specific energies that can be saddled for specific magical objectives.

WORKING WITH THE LUNAR CYCLE

The connection between magic and the Moon can be comprehensively portrayed as a cycle of waxing and melting away. As the Moon develops, we work magic for increment; as it melts away, we work magic for diminishing. So, when you're looking to bring something into your life, you work with the waxing Moon, and when you need to exile or discharge some undesirable component of your life, you work during the melting away phase.

The transitional point between these two contrary energies is the Full Moon, a time of "reap" as we celebrate what we have manifested over the principal half of the cycle. We then basically "tidy up" a short time later, identifying and discharging what is never again required during the time half of the cycle. At the New Moon, we set new expectations for the following round of manifestation, without any end in sight it goes. The musicality of this cycle can be envisioned as the cadence of the tides, which the Moon is causing.

Here are some broad recommendations for timing your magic with the phases of the Moon:

New Moon: This is the earliest reference point of the lunar cycle and a decent time for longing for what you wish to make in your life. Customarily, magic planned for starting new tasks and adventures is favored as of now. However, anything, including pulling in or expanding what you want is fitting.

Waxing Moon: This phase is the perfect time for making a move toward the objectives—really starting, on the physical plane, the activities we've expected for on the profound plane. The energy here is one of activity and anticipating the goals outward into the Universe. Magical work might be related to picking up or reinforcing organizations with others (regardless of whether they be companions, sentimental interests, or business relates) and improving physical wellbeing and general prosperity.

Full Moon: This is the most dominant phase of the whole lunar cycle. Numerous Witches find that the day of the Full Moon is the most magically intense day of the month, and may spare spellwork related to especially significant objectives for this event. Any magical objects are favored during a Full Moon custom.

Melting away Moon: This is the time to discharge the energy of outward activity and line up with the energy of internal reflection. Wiping out negative energies and encounters is the prevalent magical objective now, so spellwork planned for beating deterrents, settling clashes, and evacuating reasons for an ailment is fitting.

Dark Moon: In the days just prior to the New Moon, numerous Witches shun effectively working magic, picking instead invigorate their energy for the following waxing phase. Be that as it may, innumerable others observe the Dark Moon to be the best time for magic related to the conclusion, or bringing things full circle. There is a damaging potential to the energy now that can be saddled for discharging any karmic designs that harvest up over and over in your life, for example, those related to need, surrender, betrayal, and so forth.

CHECK OUT THE MOON FOR ENHANCED MAGIC

Relatively few individuals who are new to magic have been in the propensity for giving everyday consideration to the rhythms of the Moon's circle around the Earth. If this incorporates you, consider embracing a practice of associating with the Moon every day, regardless of whether through a formal custom or only a concise, quiet welcome.

Discover where the Moon is in its cycle and recognize this as a major aspect of your everyday practice—you can discover the Full Moon plan on the web. This will enable you to adjust to the unpretentious differences in lunar energy from the stage to stage. From New to Full, to Dark and turn to New again, the ceaseless cycle of the Moon presents numerous chances to tune into the energies of the common world and improve your spellwork.

A WICCAN GUIDE TO MAGIC AND THE LAW OF ATTRACTION:

Over the previous decade, an ever-increasing number of individuals have gotten comfortable with the expression "Law of Attraction," as books, motion pictures, and classes about this subject have been grabbing the eye of a regularly developing group of spectators.

Be that as it may, the Law of Attraction isn't only an ongoing wonder. It has been talked about by journalists and masterminds from different profound, philosophical, and mysterious foundations for a few centuries, including numerous professionals of magic. You could state that for Witches, this general fundamental rule is intrinsic to all spellwork, regardless of whether the spell caster acknowledges it or not!

WHAT IS THE LAW OF ATTRACTION?

This standard is regularly summed up as "like pulls in like," or "thoughts become things." It's a method for clarifying that the Universe reacts to your thoughts and feelings, carrying your conditions that line up with your predominant vibrational recurrence, which is dictated by your convictions about what is conceivable. For instance, have you seen that if you choose to accept that no doubt about it "awful day," encounters that match, this conviction will keep on appearing throughout the day? However, if you center during the day around positive thoughts and emotions, you will pull in positive encounters.

Numerous individuals battle with this idea, as it infers that everything that has ever transpired—regardless of whether positive or negative—is their very own consequence thoughts and convictions. This is presumably the greatest obstacle to move beyond when it comes to placing the Law of Attraction into purposeful practice in your life. For sure, there's significantly more to it than the genuinely oversimplified expression "thoughts become things" would recommend, and an exhaustive comprehension of how it truly works is past the extent of only one thought. In any case, you don't need to get a handle in general picture to make the guideline itself work for you. What's more, if you have an enthusiasm for the magical expressions, you're now well on your approach to deliberately using the Law of Attraction!

MIND GAMES: SHIFTING YOUR ATTITUDE

If you generally read about the Law of Attraction, you'll locate a differing cluster of activities and methods for shifting your thoughts and convictions to pull in what you want into your life. A large portion of these methodologies will, in general, be established in at least one of three critical devices: thankfulness, affirmation, and perception. While each is valuable all alone, it's the blend of the three that genuinely enables your brain to roll out the required improvements.

Thankfulness, likewise frequently alluded to as appreciation, is attention on what is going admirably for you, regardless of whether you're concentrating on the prompt present minute, or on your life when all is said in done. When we try posting and perceiving the positive in lives—and see the positive emotions that outcome from this center—we are consequently shifting the consideration away from the negative, placing ourselves in a spot to draw in a more significant amount of what we appreciate.

Affirmation is the demonstration of rehashing positive explanations, regardless of whether quietly or so anyone can hear, that portray the truth we're hoping to make. For instance, if you need to expand your budgetary prosperity, you may make an affirmation like this: "you have all that you need and more for a safe, copious life." If you're looking for a relationship, you may state, "you are in a sound, the adoring relationship, you're your ideal match." Affirmation requires an eagerness to "counterfeit it till you make it" by imagining that you have just manifested your objectives. It can feel somewhat senseless from the outset, yet numerous individuals have discovered that through rehashed practice, after some time, their affirmations do turn into their world.

Representation, as you may expect, is the practice of making mental photos of the conditions we want. You invest energy envisioning the house you need to live in, the fantasy occupation you're chasing, or the condition of wellbeing you're hoping to accomplish. The objective of perception is to make a striking feeling you had always wanted working out as expected, yet it includes something other than having the option to see it in your imagination—you likewise need to make the sentiment of having accomplished your craving, because this is the thing that truly starts the way toward transforming your thoughts into things.

A MAGICAL ALIGNMENT

For the Witch, it does not shock anyone that these equivalent three procedures are worked in parts of magic. Most spellwork includes a blend of gratefulness, affirmation, and representation, working together in a synergistic manner that takes into account the ideal manifestation to come through on the physical plane. Perception of the ideal result of a spell is vital to centering your goal, and valuing the result—ahead of time—is a piece of the intensity of the representation. Affirmation is the verbally expressed piece of magic, the words that whole up and "send" the activity of the work—regardless of whether you're lighting a flame, charging an apparatus, or making a charm. As you express the expressions of a spell, you are "doing what needs to be done" that you've set up by imagining and valuing the possible result.

Magic has regularly been characterized as the utilization of centered aim to realize an ideal impact, regardless of whether that impact is a deluge of cash, another relationship, an improved living circumstance, or something less unmistakable, similar to a clearer comprehension of a current issue. The individuals who work purposefully with the Law of Attraction are doing precisely the same thing. However, they might be utilizing spellwork to "help" their advancement. An accomplished Witch's comprehension of magic is considerably more perplexing than the fundamental aphorism of "thoughts become things"— there are other basic standards at work in the Universe that go further in lighting up how and why magic works. In any case, the Law of Attraction is undoubtedly part of the more significant framework, and once you have a reasonable handle of "like pulls in like," your magic will undoubtedly turn out to be increasingly viable.

THE WICCAN "BRILLIANT RULE"

Liquid as Wiccan magical practices might be, notwithstanding, there is as yet the one fundamental "rule" to remember consistently: Harm None. Taken from the Wiccan rede, this straightforward expression reminds us to be mindful to look at the thought processes and intentions when picking or making a spell.

We're not originating from a spiritual spot if we wish to work the magic that would carry adverse outcomes to someone else, period. Be that as it may, "hurt none" additionally applies to any manipulative magic, regardless of how good-natured we maybe about it. This implies we don't work magic to influence the emotions or conduct of anybody other than ourselves. We likewise don't work magic for others without their unequivocal authorization, and we never attempt to choose for others what their best advantages are.

Chapter 6 What Do Wiccans Believes

The Horned God / The Sun God

The masculine god is often seen or referred to as the horned god. Horns are a traditional symbol of masculinity, representing qualities such as strength, sex drive, and energy.

During the Wiccan year, the horned god will adopt different personalities. For half of the year he can be referred to as the Oak King and for the other half, the Holly King. He is also referred to as the Sun God who is worshipped on the Sabbat of Lughnasadh. Some Wiccans believe that these are all different gods and will worship each of them separately and other Wiccans have them all fall under the God.

The Goddess / The Triple Goddess

The Goddess is the Feminine deity. Like the horns represent the masculine god, the Goddess is represented by three phases of the moon. This is why she is also called the Triple Goddess. Each phase of the moon represents a different form of the Goddess. The waxing moon represents creation and inspiration, the full moon represents sustenance and the waning moon represents fulfillment. The three forms of the Goddess are as follows:

The Maiden - The maiden is young, full of beauty and innocence. Her future is promising and filled with potential. She is associated with beginnings and the new moon.

The Mother - The mother is experienced and mature. She is protective, nurturing and selfless.

The Crone - The crone is full of wisdom, a leader and respected. She reminds us of our mortality and that our bodies will one day return to the earth. Despite this, she does not have a negative connotation. In fact, she is seen as a guide and her wisdom can help us through difficult times.

The Wheel of the Year

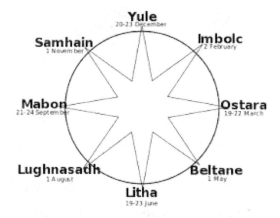

The Wheel of the Year is the Wiccan calendar if you will. It represents the annual cycle of the Earth and is derived from the seasons. Wiccans believe that time is cyclical, a continuous cycle. This is why the festivals (or Sabbats) are represented by a wheel.

The wheel also represents the progression of life. We are born, we grow, we live, we decline and then we die. This period of birth, life, and death is represented by the life of the Horned God during different seasons. The cycle of fertility (virginity, pregnancy, and birth) is represented in different seasons by the Triple Goddess.

The Sabbats

Yule: December 20-23. Yule is the winter solstice. The Goddess (in the form of the mother) gives birth to the sun god.

Imbolc: February 2. Candles are used to celebrate this Sabbat. They are to encourage the sun to shine brighter. The sun god at this stage is an infant and feeds from the breast of his mother, the Goddess. This also represents the end of winter because the earth is starting to feel the warmth of the infant sun.

Ostara: March 20-23. The spring equinox. The God is now a child, and the Goddess will take on the form of the maiden. She acts as the God's playmate and they play in the fields to encourage the flowers to bloom.

Here is where beginner Wiccans might get confused. The Goddess has now taken on two forms simultaneously. She is both the playmate of the child God (as a maiden) and the nurturing (mother) of the child. She will continue the year changing from two forms as needed in order to serve the life cycle of the God.

Beltane: May 1. The Maiden Goddess and the Sun God are now young adults. They are fertile and ready to procreate. For this reason, Beltane is viewed by Wiccans as a sacred night for sex. Fertility also represents the upcoming crops. The Sun God will impregnate the maiden here and she will turn from the maiden to the pregnant mother. The Goddess is now both the pregnant lover of the God as well as his nurturing mother.

Litha: June 20-23. The summer solstice. Litha is the peak of the Sun God's life, he is now full of strength and masculinity. Litha is when the Sun God and the pregnant Goddess will get married.

Lughnasadh: August 1. Autumn is upon the earth. The leaves are turning brown and the temperature is cooling. The Sun God is dying. The God will begin preparations for his death and make sure that his unborn child and the pregnant Goddess are taken care of. The Sun God knows that winter is upon the earth and it will be a challenge to survive it. He knows that his strength and light can only be renewed if he willingly offers himself up as a sacrifice. He will do this to become one with the earth to provide sustenance. His sacrifice will be the wheat that is harvested for the winter.

Mabon: September 20-23. Time with the Sun God has nearly ended. Preparation for his death and the winter are in full swing. Knowing of losing her son, the nurturing mother transitions into the crone. Her wisdom and experience will help guide us through the mourning of the Sun God.

Samhain: October 31. The Sun God dies. Many Wiccans believe that this is when the Sun God is referred to as the Horn God. He is animal-like, he is one with the earth.

During Samhain, the crone and the pregnant mother goddess mourn the God's death. Samhain is the start of the New Year for Wiccans and many Wiccans view Samhain as the most important Sabbat. Samhain is a day to remember those who have passed on, including ancestors, family and even animals that were either pets or used on a farm. Samhain rituals celebrate darkness.

Although it is considered the beginning of the year, it also marks the end of the previous year in which rituals celebrate and commemorate last year's harvest and the accomplishments that were made.

Samhain also represents a promise of new life. The pregnant mother holds the seed of the reincarnated Son God who will be born at Yule.

Yule: December 20-23. The Goddess gives birth and the Sun God is reborn, thus re-starting the cycle.

The Greater Sabbats and the Lesser Sabbats

The eight Sabbats are divided in half making four of them greater Sabbats and the other four, lesser Sabbats. The divide is as follows:

Greater Sabbats:

Samhain (October 31)

Imbolc (February 2)

Beltane (May 1)

Lughnasadh (August 1)

Lesser Sabbats:

Yule (December 20-23)

Ostara (March 20-23)

Litha (June 20-23)

Mabon (September 20-23)

The four lesser Sabbats mark the end of one season and the beginning of the next while the four greater Sabbats are the middle or the peak of the season. These days are considered days of power.

Esbats

Although the Goddess plays a key role in each of the Sabbats, they are mostly used to outline the life cycle of the God or the sun. The Goddess is represented by the moon, as she is the polar opposite of the God. Therefore, we celebrate the Goddess during **Esbats** which follow the phases of the moon rather than the sun.

As a reminder, the Triple Goddess is represented by three phases of the moon. The maiden is represented by the waxing moon, the mother by the full moon and the crone by the waning moon. Esbats take place whenever the moon is full, which means they occur twelve or thirteen times a year.

The Blue Moon Esbat

During each solar year, there will be either twelve or thirteen full moons. The thirteenth full moon (or Esbat) will occur once every two and a half years and this is referred to as the "blue moon". This Esbat is rare and is considered to have more power and energy than a regular Esbat. The presence of the Goddess during the blue moon is very powerful and is a great time for beginner witches or Wiccans to establish a connection with her. The blue moon is a time that Wiccans find very sacred and they will hold special rituals under the light of the blue moon.

My First Blue Moon Ritual

The first time I held my own blue moon ritual was truly astounding. See, as a Christian, I had never had a spiritual experience with a feminine deity. Since I am a woman, I always felt that side of my spiritual being was missing from my religious faith.

I went outside to perform my ritual under the moonlight and called upon the Goddess, hoping that I would be able to feel her presence. Although I couldn't feel her right away, a few minutes (or maybe an hour?) in and I knew she was there with me. I could feel her telling me that I was not lesser or weaker because I was not a man.

Without her power, the God would not exist and I felt myself understanding my role as a woman on this earth. Motherhood, fertility and nurturing kindness were all equally as important as strength, the need to provide and masculinity. If you are a woman, I highly recommend taking part in a ritual under the full moon. You will feel an overwhelming sense of belonging and understanding of your place on this earth.

If you are a man, I recommend performing this ritual even more. See masculine and feminine energy aren't limited to one gender or the other. There is a feminine side to you and if you have grown up Christian, that side of your being has likely been ignored for years. Making time to appreciate the Goddess and how her feminine energy lives inside you will help make you truly whole. At least that is my theory on the matter, every Wiccan is free to take their own path.

Reincarnation

Unlike Christians, Wiccans do not believe in the idea of heaven and hell but we do believe in an afterlife, or a place where the soul can live without the physical body.

As a witch on this earth, your purpose is to better yourself, better your environment and help others. You are to go through life's ups and downs, learn from your mistakes, collect wisdom and grow as a person. This is the same purpose that your soul has.

Your soul is meant to experience the physical world, die, reflect on the life it lived and then be reincarnated into a new physical life. The goal is that each physical life is lived better than the last. For this reason, we can assume that people who are immoral and treat others badly are "new souls" who have not yet lived many lives and learned how to be good.

The Afterlife

Every time your soul lives a life and reflects upon it in The Afterlife, it will live a more moral and spiritually satisfying physical life the next time it is reincarnated. It's like your soul is on a mission to live the perfect physical life and it takes numerous tries for this to happen.

So, what is the Afterlife? The Afterlife is a place (similar to the idea of heaven) where your soul can go and rest before it is reincarnated into a new physical body. Unlike heaven, however, this place is not a place where your soul will be judged. While you are in The Afterlife, you can communicate with the other souls, the deities and reflect on the physical life you just lived. If you lived a bad life, you will follow the guidance of the Goddess and the God in hopes that your next life will be more spiritually satisfying. Once your soul has satisfied the physical life's purpose, it will remain in The Afterlife for all eternity.

The God and Goddess (or Lord and Lady)

Wicca acknowledges both the masculine god and the feminine goddess. They both represent unique but essential characteristics and are seen as equal. Now for Christians, the deities in Wicca can be confusing, I know it was for me! This is because Christianity focuses on a very rigid set of beliefs but Wiccans have the ability to interpret things on their own.

Some Wiccans view the God and Goddess as two gods. Other Wiccans believe there are many different masculine deities which collectively would be referred to as the God or Horned God and that there would also be many feminine deities that all together would be referred to as the Goddess or Triple Goddess.

To compare this to Christianity, we can use God, Jesus, and the Holy Spirit. In Christianity you would consider all three of those entities to be "God" but they can either be broken down into individual entities or referred to as a whole.

In Wicca, you have the ability to choose whether you want to refer to the God and Goddess as a whole or if you'd like to worship the individual deities and break them down further. I will outline the basic overview of the God and Goddess but I recommend delving deeper into this on your own.

Other Beliefs

The Rule of Three

The rule of Threefold means that whatever energies we put into the universe, it will be returned to us times three. This can include every day acts of kindness or negativity or a lifetime of treating people or a person in a certain way. Wiccans who do not practice magick or witchcraft still abide by the rule by the actions they choose to do and the decisions they make every day of their lives.

For Wiccans who **do** practice witchcraft, this rule becomes even more significant. Once you are able to create spells and harness your powers, you will be able to cause things to happen to people. You can use this power for good or bad but the Threefold rule states that whatever we put out into the world; it will come back to us threefold so mind what you do as it will come back to you.

The Elements

The elements are integral parts of Wicca. The elements: earth, wind, water, and fire are seen as the components that make up the earth as well as energies that make up living beings. This means that they are considered the root of all matter. The elements are often a large part of rituals and are used in their physical forms to purify a ritual circle.

Fire:

Fire is an integral part of a comfortable human existence but we do not necessarily need it to survive. Fire gives us warmth in the cold, allows us to cook food and is a source of light in the darkness. For these reasons we should look to fire less as a survival element and more of a luxury in which we should offer our deepest gratitude. Fire is also one of the more dangerous elements and should always be treated with caution and respect.

Fire is used in candle magic and also to create an environment for rituals and spellwork. In rituals, fire is represented in the form of burning objects, baking and lighting candles or bonfires.

Symbol:

Deity: The Sun God

Energy: Masculine (to will)

Tools: Candles, bonfire

Season: **Summer**

Corresponding Zodiac Signs: **Aries, Leo, Sagittarius**

Air:

Air is a symbol of our intelligence and our ability to communicate with other humans on this earth as well as the spirits. Air is how some Wiccans have psychic powers and telepathy.

Unlike fire, air is crucial to our survival and reminds us of the importance of being connected with both earthly beings as well as spiritual beings. It reminds that we are very fragile and we can be transferred to the afterlife if we are without air for only a few minutes.

Air is used in rituals by tossing objects into the wind, burning incense of aromatic candles. Air is used in spells that involve freedom, knowledge, traveling and psychic powers.

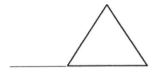

Symbol:

Deity: The Sun God

Energy: Masculine (to will)

Tools: Wand, incense, bell

Season: **Spring**

Corresponding Zodiac Signs: **Gemini, Libra, Aquarius**

Water:

Water is the most versatile of the elements. It can be present in the form of a liquid, solid and gas and each of those states can be used to excerpt different magical qualities of water. Water is an integral part of our lives and is used to nourish ourselves as well as the earth in the form of plants and animals.

Water is a symbol of the subconscious, purification, wisdom and emotions. It is the element of love and femininity. In rituals, water is represented by pouring water over objects, making brews, and ritual bathing.

Symbol:

Deity: The Triple Goddess

Energy: Feminine (to listen)

Tools: Cauldron, cups

Season: Autumn

Corresponding Zodiac Signs: **Pisces, Cancer, Scorpio**

Earth:

Earth is the foundation upon which all is built. As Wiccans, we take pride in our relationship with the earth and consider the earth a direct pathway to the divine. The more we take care of our earth, the more we honor the God and Goddess. The earth is a symbol of life. All life is born of the earth, grows and is nourished by the earth and then returns to the earth in death. The earth represents strength, abundance, prosperity, and femininity. In rituals, the earth is represented by salt, burying items in the ground, herbalism and crystals.

Symbol:

Deity: The Triple Goddess

Energy: Feminine (to listen)

Tools: Pentacle, a bowl of salt

Season: Winter

Corresponding Zodiac Signs: **Taurus, Virgo, Capricorn**

Wiccan Symbols

Just like Christians have the cross, Wiccans also have symbols that represent different aspects of the faith. Although there are many, I will cover the four main ones below.

Pentacle:

The pentacle is a pentagram within a circle. It is the most common and traditional symbol of Wicca.

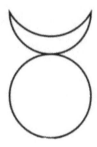

The Horned God:

This symbol represents the masculine God as we can see his horns above his body. The horned God is also known as the Sun God.

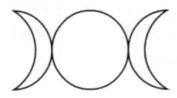

The Triple Goddess:

This symbol represents the Triple Goddess with the phases of the moon representing each of her forms.

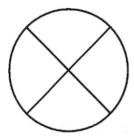

Wheel:

This symbol represents the wheel of the year, and a cyclical view of time rather than linear. Each piece represents one of the eight Sabbats.

Chapter 7 Life-Changing Moon Manifesting Visualization Strategy

After you have a clear intention set and you've got your mind, body, soul and environment on board, you will used advanced, but easy visualizations to enhance the energy of the goal.

Using visualization techniques and repeating powerful affirmations, along with the energy of the moon- we supercharge our dreams and wishes at an even more accelerated rate!

If you can see it in your mind, you can hold it in your hand. Visualization is comparable to a super power! When using the moon to crush your goals, we will use science based, strategic visualizations to trick your brain and bring these goals into fruition quickly!

When it comes to our visualizations two things are important-First, we must fast forward in our mind, and imagine ourselves living in the moment as if the goal were already true. We want to visualize how the situation looks once we have attained the goal!

So, if your goal is to have more self-worth, you will imagine and visualize yourself going to the gym every day, raising your hand in a meeting with confidence, or seeing yourself eating healthy and taking care of yourself.

If you want to manifest a promotion- you will visualize yourself having a meeting with your boss, hearing the great news, moving into your new office, and imagine your pay increase by visualizing massive deposits coming to your bank account!

Do you get it? Your goal is to make your intention as real as possible in your mind. The more detail you can picture the better! You can even write this visualization down and hang it, or place it next to your intention paper.

The second most important part of visualization is feeling the feelings and emotions your intention will bring you. How will it feel when you're self-worth is back? How will it feel when you've finally gotten the promotion you've been working so hard for? It's going to feel damn good! So, the last part of our visualization we FEEL!

You will picture yourself feeling proud that with your promotion you can finally afford to take your family on vacation. You will feel happy that financial stress has been removed from your life. You will feel your confidence build and feel feelings of joy that your self-worth is back!

It doesn't matter what your goal may be- you really want to get deep into the feelings and emotions that will come with this newly attained goal.

So now that you've set your intention, have a good visualization of that intention, and have brainstormed on all the feelings that intention will bring with it- you're ready to put everything together and complete your Moon Manifesting Visualization exercise.

90 second Moon Manifesting Visualization

Sit or lay down in a quiet space.

Close your eyes.

Take a few deep breaths and release any tension in the body.

Picture a funnel at the top of your head and imagine a white light pouring through it, and into your body.

Imagine this light filling your entire body from head to toe, covering every part of your body until every cell is illuminated. Image this light is swirling within you and around you, as if you're floating in a white bubble of powerful energy.

Picture yourself walking down an illuminated path that is leading you to your intention or goal

Arrive at a real-life scenario where you've obtained the goal.

How does this goal look? What are you doing? Who are you with? What can you see, taste, smell and touch? Make this goal as real as possible in your mind- visualizing as many aspects as you can.

Visualize the moment you receive your intention.

How does this intention FEEL? How does it feel to have it? Run through at least 3 feelings and emotions. Smile and make it as real as possible!

Show gratitude and appreciation for this vision and affirm that you know it will be true for you at the perfect time.

Float back to earth enriched by your vision.

Lock in the feeling of power, and know that you are in control of your life, and you have the power to make this happen!

You are going to do this exercise for 90 seconds every morning, and 90 seconds every night before going to bed. The most effective time to visualize is first thing in the morning and right before bed, so of course, you are going to do just that!

You dream deserve 180 seconds per day! This exercise will not only help you attain your goal- it will uplift your spirit, set a positive tone for your day and help you sleep better at night!

Crafting Your Master Plan

Next, we must make a strategic plan that will lead us closer to our intention.

What can we bring in, or let go of in order to be totally ready to receive this intention? How serious are you about this goal? For goals to bloom they must first start with intention, and planning is the next extremely important factor.

What steps can you take to set up your environment? What small actions can you take immediately, and what big actions can you already sense will be necessary? Think about all of the things you may have to do now, and start immediately.

Create your plan the last night of the new moon or the first night of the waxing moon. Remember, each phase has 3 days.

In this phase, we don't have to exactly know *how* we are going to get there- but we have to plan out *some* milestones in order for the goal to be fully attained. Don't worry about every step, you will be guided once you start taking action.

For example, if your dream is to get a promotion, and you have only thought and visualized about it, but haven't planned or set yourself up for success- the goal will not align.

You are a magnet, you are constantly attracting and bringing different situations into your life. If you want a promotion, you've got to set the intention, visualize on it and then you must make a plan to speak with your supervisor about it. Set a date, decide what you will say to your boss and plant the seed in your bosses' mind that you're interested.

A second part of your plan could look like gathering all your latest work to show your boss at that meeting, and then schedule a follow-up to seal the deal a few weeks down the road.

An important note to remember, your plan needs to align with the energy of the moon and her phases. Your worst-case scenario would be setting a date to meet with your Supervisor to show you are the candidate for that new high paying position on the Balsamic Moon when energy is null.

Set the date during the New or Waxing phase, and catch your boss when the energy is momentous. When you start planning and scheduling important dates with the moon- your life will transform in ways you did not think were possible.

All of the fine details will work themselves out, doors will start opening and leading you to your goal, but you have got to plan the essential stepping stones you know need to happen to make this baby work!

Planning is essential for any goal to manifest. Plan out a few steps you can take right now and get started right away!

Pro tip: When it comes to manifesting- don't worry about the little details, just focus on the end goal working out perfectly and the steps you need to take to get there. When you take action on your plan, time it with the moon and trust that the energy from the universe is helping you- nothing can stop it from manifesting!

Waxing Moon: Taking Action

Next, we must act on our plans. We must start showing the moon and the universe that we mean business! The energy during the waxing moon is momentous, forward moving and energetic.

These two weeks are a busy time, and really the only two weeks of the month you have to take strategic action.

After setting the intention, visualizing the shit out of it, and crafting your plan- you have to take massive action.

I wish it was so easy, we could set our intention, say a few affirmations, and wallah- it's here! But, unfortunately, this is not how the universe works people. We have to act in order to receive.

We have to show intent and act upon that intent for this system to truly work. Start taking small steps and use this phase to your advantage. The sooner you act, the sooner you shall receive.

Remember to continue practicing your moon manifesting visualization every morning, and every night. The universe works in laws and by visualizing every day, you are using the law of attraction to attract your goal to you rapidly.

Full Moon: Gratitude & Release

The full moon is where we pause, reflect and have a moment of gratitude for how far we've come. WOW, We're doing it. We're making changes, doing the work and each day we are getting closer!

For some of you, you may have never dug this deep into a goal. So, it's time to be thankful and pat yourself on the back.

During the full moon everything is illuminated the good, the bad, the bittersweet, and the ugly. The energy during the full moon asks us not only to be grateful, but to become aware of what isn't working, and release it from lives for good.

It may be part of the plan that needs to go, or it may be a toxic person holding you back, or even an old belief that keeps you stuck. Whatever it is- thank it for what it was worth and let that shit go!

If you are serious about your moon manifesting mission- you must let go and create space for your new manifestation. If toxic people or toxic thoughts are holding you back, the universe will not deliver.

Let go. Release it forever. Say good-bye. You are blooming into the person you want to become and you have no time for heavy energy holding you down.

I recommend performing a Full Moon ritual, taking a bath and sitting outside under the full moon and releasing what needs to go under this energy.

Waning Moon: Reflect & Revamp the Plan

The two weeks of the waning moon, energy is decreasing, slow moving and can almost feel overwhelming, chaotic and confusing. Remember, this is not the time we are beginning ANYTHING new.

These are two weeks we are analyzing the plan- tweaking and changing what we can to do more, to do better on the next moon cycle. In this phase we are looking deep into ourselves, tuning in, and allowing the universe to guide us. Our goal is to stay in tune with the flow and energy of the moon and universe.

You need to really become aware during this phase. Become aware of your thoughts, your feelings and make sure your goal still aligns with your vibe and purpose.

You need to become aware of what's working and what isn't. So many times, we hold onto things in our lives that weren't meant for us. If your plan feels hard or uninteresting, maybe it isn't for you!

More often than not, people find that what they thought they wanted, wasn't for them, and things change. If this is the case for you- that is okay! Move on and start anew, with a new goal, on the next new moon.

On the other side- You may be feeling more passionate about your goal then ever! Signs and synchronities may have already started appearing in your life, or some of you may already be living your dream.

Wherever you are is perfect. You just need to reflect, weed out the weeds and water the flowers now during the waning moon.

Balsamic Moon: Treat Yo' Self

Balsamic actually comes from the word *"balsam"* which means to soothe or relax, and this is exactly what this phase is all about. The balsamic, or dark moon phase is the last phase of the cycle and the energy is asking us to let go of all worry, and pause our actions, and to just melt into total relaxation.

These three days where we are in total chill, no f*cks, no stress type of mood! These are three days of the month where total self-love and self-care is first priority!

Some people may find these three days very tough, as most of us do not put ourselves first or set time aside for self-love each month. Others may wish this phase was longer. However, you feel- you should schedule a solo soothing activity or plan to veg out at home.

Take a bubble bath, infuse it with essential oils and crystals, light some candles and let your body, mind and soul totally let go. Get a massage, acupuncture, go on a meditation retreat, or take a walk in nature. Allow yourself to be free from your phone and "reality" as much as you can during this phase.

When we give ourselves space from our goal and slow down for a moment, we allow a re-set to happen on a subconscious level. When we begin again on the new moon, we will feel energized, recharged and motivated to keep going.

Life is all about balance, and if you really want to achieve your goals, you have to relax. If you keep going and going, you will get totally burnt out! This is why we must take a break, each cycle, each moon, each month.

Rinse & Repeat

You made it through your first moon cycle and first intention cycle!!! Pat yourself on the back and be proud- you are aligning and becoming one with the abundance of the universe. You may have already attained your goal in just one cycle, but for most of us this won't be the case.

As I said earlier, where ever you are is perfect. When the next new moon arrives, it's go time! You've revised your plan; you've taken a break and It's time to jump back into action.

Start fresh each new moon and repeat this step by step strategy until you make it happen! Your goals may take time to manifest, the universe will only deliver when you are totally ready. You have to be ready in your inner world, your other world, and have unshakeable faith that your dream will come true for you!

It's essential you follow all of the steps in this book, accordingly. If you do not visualize, if you do not set a clear intention with a clear plan, and if you do not take action- there is no way it's going to happen!

A dream is just a dream without action, faith and imagination. If you dream big, work hard and believe in yourself- anything is possible.

Chapter 8 Candle Magic Guide

Different colored candles are used for different spells because of their meanings. When you look at a yellow color, you feel happy, and when you think of the color green you usually associate it with nature or money. The same concept is applied to candles and their colors. Each color has a different vibration and frequency which matches different spells.

For example, blue is associated with meditation, calmness within the body and healing of fevers, cuts, and bruises. Since the blue's properties match the vibrations of the blue candle, you can't expect to heal a fever with the yellow candle that has a completely different vibration.

When spell casting, it is important you first determine your goal and what spell you are casting before choosing the correct candle. Each candle is also associated with a specific day of the week which can aid in enhancing the power of the spell, energy, and intentions. Now, although, if you cast a spell on a different day than stated, it still has a pretty good chance to work out, it is recommended you cast a spell on it's said day below unless the spell instructions state otherwise. It is important for the spell to activate its full power and with good intentions, it can succeed.

Black candles can help fight evil. They have a strong power to banish negativity, a person, or spirits from your life. These candles do not represent bad luck, instead, they are associated with universe's healing energy, forgiveness and moving on from different situations, and it can help leave behind old troubles. Cast spells on a Saturday, during a waning Moon if using this candle.

White candles represent purity, protection, white magic, and blessings. This is also the only candle that can be used to substitute any other candle in spells. It is mostly used in spells regarding a change, marriage, birth, cleansing, healing emotionally, and peace. The white candle represents the Moon, and spells using this candle should be cast on Monday.

Purple candles are associated with enhancing psychic powers, intuition, and your vision through your third eye chakra. It can cancel out bad luck or bad karma within a person or yourself. The purple candle can aid in accessing knowledge or wisdom regarding the higher realms, and the usage this candle should be cast on a Thursday. Physically, this candle can cure allergies and colds.

Blue candles are the most spiritual and healing candles. It can help clear mental fog, doubts, or uncertainty, and bring peace and harmony to the mind. This is a spiritual candle, anything involving your higher self, astral travel, meditation, or any spiritual troubles should use this candle on a Thursday.

Physically the blue candles can heal almost anything from fevers, bruises, cuts, blood pressure, headaches, woman problems, and insomnia.

Green candles are associated with money, good fortune, nature, financial affairs, and good luck. It is a rich candle, and not just in terms of money. If casting spells regarding marriage, add the green candle to enhance love and provide good luck. Involving green candles, cast the spell on a Friday. Physically, the green candle can heal colds, woman problems, and headaches.

Red candles represent love, passion, and lust. They are mostly used when casting spells relating to romance, soulmates, or sexual desires. The red candle can also be used for purification, bravery, courage, and inspiration. This candle represents strong emotions and should be cast on a Tuesday.

Yellow candles symbolize the mind, creativity, focus, inspiration, visualization, and memory. Often, this candle is used to help pass a test and invoke memory. It can also represent good luck, happiness, prosperity, and can be used in divination work. The yellow candles should be used on a Wednesday. Physically, this candle can cure indigestion and diabetes.

Orange candles are the action energy needed to achieve goals. This candle can help with sexual attraction, creativity, enthusiasm, sex magic, good luck, gaining control, courage, and weight loss. Anything involving the law or business is associated with the orange candle. Casting such spells should be done on a Sunday, in the middle of the day when the sun is strong. Orange candles can also help heal depression.

Pink candles are the purer version of the red candles. Instead of passionate romance, this candle can help attract your other half into your life. It's an innocent color involving friendships, stability, purification, self-love, travel, and new beginnings. If you are looking for a change, then this candle is for you. Pink candles should be used on a Friday. Physically, pink candles can help heal anxiety and depression.

Silver candles are associated with the Moon goddess. It represents mental clarity, awareness, astral realm, intuition, insight, and can help communicate with spirits and ancestors. This color is also connected with love, psychic abilities, healing, and dream magic. This candle should be burned on a Monday.

Gold candles can help you answer questions, or guide you on your destined path. They also represent protection, good fortune, skills, success, and security. The color gold itself represents money and wealth and casting spells on a Sunday with a gold candle can help you attract money and financial success into your life.

Brown candles are associated with nature, grounding yourself, earth magic, stability, nurturing, balance, and healing. It can aid in communicating with nature and animals. Brown candles represent the Mother Earth and when connecting to the element of earth, you should use this candle to strengthen the connection. Cast spells using this candle on a Monday, Friday, or Saturday.

Candle colors are just one layer of candle magic. Essential oils, herbs, and sigils are other layers that are not necessary but can help enhance the power of the spells and the intentions.

Sigils

Sigils should be carved first before applying any essential oils. Sigils are powerful symbols or signs that can enhance the spell. For example, if you are casting a spell on protection, you will need a protection sigil, carved into the candle. You can always just carve the word itself, but sigils can enhance the intentions. There are many different and popular sigils online, below are some of the most basic and common sigils for different spells and rituals.

Symbol	Meaning	Symbol	Meaning	Symbol	Meaning	Symbol	Meaning
	Air		God		Money		Cause sleep
	Deadly		Goddess		Mother		Spirituality
	Blessing		Health		Peace		Spring
	Crone		Lose weight		Pentacle		Summer
	Deosil		Love		Pentagram		Travel
	Earth		Magick circle		Protect child		Water
	Fall		Magick energy		Protection		Widdershins
	Fertility		Magick strength		Pyshic awareness		Winter
	Fire		Maiden		Purification		Witch
	Friendship		Marriage		Rebirth		Yonic

You can always make your own sigil and design it however you seem fit, this gives it more energy and charges it. Sigils can also be written on a piece of paper, drawn in notebooks, or even sewed on pillowcases to promote a good night's rest. Once you've finished carving it, activate it by placing your hands on the candle, or whatever you put the sigil on, visualize yourself feeling protected, for example, if that was your sigil, and simply connect your energy through your fingers and to the sigil.

Essential Oils

There are so many different essential oils and each of them has a different and unique ability. Essential oils are just another layer used to cleanse and charge the candle in order to purify it and give it all the necessary energy to carry out your intentions into the world. Below are some of the basic essential oils for candles and what they are used for.

Love - **Cyclamen, Rose, Gardenia, and Jasmin oils**

Concentration - **Honeysuckle, Rosemary, and Lilac oils**

Fertility - **Musk and Vervain oils**

Protection - **Cypress, Rose, Rosemary, and Geranium oils**

Courage - **Iris, and Musk oils**

Meditation - **Hyacinth, Magnolia, Acacia, and**

Jasmine oils

Harmony - **Gardenia, Basil, and Lilac oils**

Money - **Mint, Vervain, Honeysuckle, and Bayberry oil**

Healing - **Sandalwood, Myrrh, Rosemary, and Lotus oils**

There are also two main ways to properly dress a candle with essential oil. Put some oil on the tip of your fingers, not too much. If you want to attract something into your life such as love, money, or luck, you have to rub the candle downward, from the top to the middle of the candle while setting your intentions. If you wish to abolish or banish something from your life, then rub the candle in a downward motion, from the middle to the bottom. Remember to never rub a candle back and forth, it can cancel out any intentions that you are setting.

Herbs

Herbs are another layer which is often added after applying essential oil onto the candle and just like essential oils, each is used for a different purpose. Below are a few of the main herbs used on candles that can be found in your kitchen.

Basil is used for love, business success, peace, happiness, and money. Physically, it can heal a headache, reduce anxiety, act as an antibiotic, and even prevent flatulence.

Chili powder is used in spells to ward off unwanted or negative energies or boost the energy of the spell. Physically, it can act as an antioxidant and help reduce fat.

Cloves are used to stop gossip, promote strong protection from evil and promote wealth. Physically, it can help reduce toothache pain, inflammation, and even an aphrodisiac.

Black pepper is used for banishing, binding, exorcism, and protection from unwanted or negative energy. Physically, it can help heal from the flu or a cold and can aid in digestion.

Cinnamon can deliver fast money, wealth, healing, happiness, and love. Physically, it can reduce stress and prevent car sickness.

Rosemary is used for healing, blessing, love, and purification. Physically, it can help relieve a sore throat.

Salt is the most common herb which can help purify, cleanse or heal the body, mind, and soul. Physically, it can help reduce sinus swelling.

Tips and Tricks

Always remember that a white candle can be used to substitute any candles and, in any spells, because it absorbs all the colors, but reflects none.

Always cleanse and clean your candles when you get them from a store. Candles are known to pick up other vibrations from different objects or people, and you never know if those vibrations are good or bad. Always remember to cleanse your candles when you first bring them into your home and before you start casting spells.

Candles should not be blown out, that often is like an insult to the element of fire. You can always use your wet finger to put out the flame, or if you are too scared then a toll can help. Simply covering the candle and cutting out its oxygen can also help put it out but be careful to not burn anything down.

It is not necessary, but during spell work, many practitioners let their candles be burned down all the way to ensure that the wish has been heard loud and clear through the smoke of the candle.

When you attempt to light the candle and for some reason, it doesn't light up, it means that right now is not the right time to be casting this spell. You are either not mentally ready or there is something going on around you, some unknown force is trying to stop you or help you. In this case, carefully think through what could be the problem or the solution.

When the candle goes out during your spell work, it can also mean that something is interfering with your work. If it's a negative energy interfering, then you should immediately cast a protection spell and banish it.

Beeswax candles are known to be the most powerful candles.

You can always make your own candles from a couple of ingredients while doing so, the candles catch on to your positive vibrations which helps unite the energy when casting spells.

When looking or gazing into the candle flame, you can strengthen and focus your intentions. It can also be used as a substitute for meditation if you are in a rush.

Different colored candles have different purposes, if you use the wrong colored candle for a spell then you can get completely different results from what you asked for or in another scenario, the spell can backfire on you and make everything worse. Follow instructions of the spell carefully to see which color to use or if you are casting your own spell, take some time to determine which candle would suit the spell best.

Chapter 9 The months of the year and the days of the week, correlations with the moon

As you continue to delve deeper into understanding Wicca, you will learn about covens and circles and the difference between them and solitary practice. You will also discover that it is quite tasking to directly access other Wicca practitioners. This is because there is no central place of worship where, as a beginner, you can go to seek insight and guidance.

"Coven" is a Latin word that means to "meet up." It was widely used during the Middle Ages to describe social gatherings of different types. In the early 1600s, covens were more associated with witches. Covens gained further popularity in the mid-20th century as the "Old Religion" was being re-introduced.

A coven was initially a 13-member of witches who secretly met to practice. A coven was comprised of a High Priest and a High Priestess who spoke to the God and the Goddess. Today, however, covens do not necessarily have to have 13 members. Different Wiccans were initiated into the tradition following either the belief systems of Alex Sanders or Gerald Gardner. Some Wiccan covens will follow the initial traditions while others embrace different varied beliefs.

Most Wiccan covens have a set-out tradition of initiating new members into the coven. These set-out traditions are custom and the coven requires the new members to fully invest themselves in the initiation. Once the new member is initiated, other requirements follow to ascertain the new member's commitment to the coven. There are different levels of initiation and the new members follow certain custom conditions to get from the first to the third degree. The prerequisites to progress from one degree to another are dependent on the coven a member is following.

As a common practice, a Wiccan coven will mark the Sabbats and Esbats celebrations. Others will also mark other days between these two celebrations. For these celebrations, if a coven intends to include a new member, then they will invest their time and energy into getting the individual ready. Members of the same coven are family to one another. The members have a very close bond. Therefore, when a coven intends to welcome a new individual, all the members are invested in the process including the individual in question.

If you are a beginner in Wicca, it is highly unlikely that you will immediately join a coven. This is because most covens require one to have been practicing for more than a year especially before you can go through the initiation process. This is a great requirement because it ensures that the individual is fully certain and committed to being part of a Wiccan coven. Understandably so, if joining a coven is difficult for you, you might consider finding other practicing Wiccans within your locale and joining their circle or you could simply start your own circle.

A circle is a gathering of individuals who are Wiccan practitioners. They meet to talk and explore the Craft. It could conceivably include a normal Sabbat and additionally Esbat celebration. However, on the off chance that these occasions are marked, participation is common but not compulsory.

Contingent upon the general inclinations of the gathering, there might be numerous individuals, some of whom drop in and out as it suits them, or only a couple of consistently included companions. The structure of a circle is commonly free and doesn't require official inception or include a setup chain of importance. Amateurs are regularly welcome, and you're probably going to locate a wide scope of information and experience levels around, where everybody contributes their very own point of view.

If you can't locate any similarly invested people in your general vicinity, don't be concerned. There are numerous online networks of Wiccans and different Witches to study, and there are likewise numerous advantages to solo practice. Actually, by far most of the Wiccans in the 21st century are solo practitioners. Becoming more acquainted with the otherworldly and mystical parts of the Universe all alone can be extremely fulfilling!

In case you're sure you need to work with others, be that as it may, you can approach the Goddess and God to attract the opportune individuals to you. At that point be tolerant, trust divine planning, and your coven or circle will, in the end, show up in your life.

As a solo practitioner, we can explore how you can initiate and dedicate yourself to the practice. A custom of self-commitment may look like parts of a coven initiation to changing degrees, but since single Witches can structure and play out this custom in any capacity they like, it is on a very basic level diverse experience.

Self-dedication happens entirely without having to conform to anyone else terms. The dedication you're announcing in such a custom is true to your internal identity, or to any gods you may join into your training, and to the heavenliness of the Universe as you comprehend it. It is anything but a promise to some other individual, or passage into a gathering of individual experts. What's more, since this experience is entirely among you and the universe, you can consider it whatever you like—initiation, self-commitment, self-initiation, or something different completely, if that is the thing that sounds good to you.

In spite of the fact that this is an altogether different ordeal from that of a coven initiation, there are still critical parallels on the adventure to this achievement nonetheless. In the first place, obviously, is crafted by truly figuring out the Craft—investigating conceivable roads as far as learning customs, getting a sense of what impacts you and what doesn't, and proceeding to seek information to any extent you feel applicable and as broadly as possible. It's generally prescribed to go through a year and multi-day contemplating the Craft before attempted your self-initiation, yet you can positively take longer on the off chance that you understand the process.

When you feel prepared to step toward initiation, you can begin contemplating what this will mean to you.

In case you find yourself interested, you can take parts of one practice and other parts from another, making up your own way toward Wicca practice. Yet, you can at present concentrate on learning as you work your way toward the point where you feel prepared for initiation. You can "allocate" yourself a specific measure of study every week and arrange your investigations around explicit themes. For example, the Triple Goddess or the Wheel of the Year, and additionally peruse every one of the books composed by a specific writer before proceeding onward to another one. On the other hand, you might find that you are interested in a diversity of books, following your intuition so that you are able to grasp from these books the information you feel is relevant to you.

With regards to the Wiccan initiation custom itself, you can structure your own process of initiation. Simply realize that the subtleties are less critical than your genuine want to formalize your pledge to the Wiccan lifestyle. You can even ask the Goddess and God to enable you to pick your best method.

Self-dedication is an individual choice that nobody can make for you, except if you are looking for enrollment in a coven. It's really a completely discretionary thing. In any case, regardless of where you look for initiation, realize that a solitary custom won't abruptly launch you into an out and out mystical presence, or certification that you'll remain on this specific route for eternity. There are Witches who have worked for their entire lives without experiencing initiation, and a lot of beginners who lost enthusiasm for Wicca did not follow through. For a long time during the initial phases, it will be dependent upon you to keep choosing your way, in your own particular manner and at your very own pace.

Wicca is regularly thought of as an approximately organized or even totally unstructured custom which is quite deep and for some individuals who were brought up in progressively formal composed religions, this is certainly part of the charm. In any case, there is a central component of Wicca that serves to unite individuals around an aggregate center, which is made up of Wiccan customs.

Regardless of whether the event is a Sabbat, an Esbat or an achievement, for example, a handfasting (wedding), an inception, or an end of-life service, covens and circle individuals will accumulate to share their love and respect of the Goddess and God, and commend the initiation to be found in the continuous cycles of life. While most Wiccan ceremonies are held in private, a few covens will once in a while hold theirs out in the open, with the goal that all who wish to watch can come and get familiar with the Craft. Numerous Wiccan circles do likewise, and may even welcome general society to take an interest.

Obviously, solo ceremonies are no less noteworthy, and singular Wiccans realize that as they venerate at each point along the Wheel of the Year, they are including their own light and capacity to the group otherworldly energy on these exceptional events.

Beautiful and mysterious, Wiccan ceremonies can take various structure, with no two occasions being actually similar. Some might be very organized and elaborate. This is frequently the situation with coven ceremonies. However, since most covens keep the subtleties of their customs secret - known only by initiated individuals - it's hard to portray them with much precision. Different ceremonies, especially those by single and varied Wiccans, might be genuinely basic by comparison, and may even be made up on the spur of the moment.

The substance of some random Wiccan custom will rely upon the event. For instance, Esbats, or Full Moon festivities, are centered exclusively upon the Goddess, while Sabbats respect the co-inventive connection between the Goddess and the God. In spite of all the conceivable varieties, nonetheless, there are a couple of essential components that will, in general, be incorporated into what we may call an "ordinary" custom.

To start with, there is decontamination, both of the celebrant(s) and where the custom is held. This can occur as a custom shower, as well as a smirching service to expel any undesirable energies from the custom space, regardless of whether it's an outside region or inside the home. Smearing includes the consuming of consecrated herbs, for example, sage, rosemary or lavender.

Setting up the altar happens first. A few Wiccans can keep a raised area permanently set up in their homes. However, even in this situation, it will probably be enriched contrastingly relying upon the event, for example, getting fall foliage for Mabon (the Autumn Equinox) or Samhain (otherwise called Halloween.) The special stepped area is part of the different Wiccan customs and will be decorated in accordance with the event that is being celebrated.

Next comes the casting of the circle, an action that sets a limit between the spiritual realm and the mundane physical world. The altar is normally the focal point of the circle, with a lot of space for all required to work unreservedly inside the circle, with no incidental venturing outside of the boundary, which is thought to contain energy. The circle might be set apart with ocean salt in a long line, a few stones, herbs or candles. There are numerous techniques for circle-casting that you will discover for yourself as you practice.

When the circle is cast, the ritual starts. The invocations here can change, yet ordinarily the God and Goddess are invited to join the ritual and afterward, the four Elements—Earth, Air, Fire, and Water—are summoned (In numerous customs, a fifth Element—Akasha, or Spirit—is additionally brought in.) In different conventions, this invocation, known as calling the Quarters, and the four bearings (North, East, South and West), is tended to, either rather than or notwithstanding the Elements.

When these actions have occurred, the core of the celebration starts. To begin with, the aim of the ceremony is expressed— regardless of whether it's to praise a Sabbat or an Esbat, or maybe to pray to the God and Goddess for the benefit of somebody who needs it or some other sort of help.

After the intention is expressed, the fundamental body of the custom may comprise of different exercises. The point of convergence might be the execution of a custom dramatization. For example, reenacting scenes from antiquated legends or sonnets—or other ritualistic material, contingent upon the convention of Wicca the gathering is following. Single Wiccans may likewise peruse from old enchanted messages, or make their very own verse for the event. Reciting, singing, moving as well as other ceremonial motions might form a part of the ceremony, and the season in which the ceremony is held will have great significance. Supplications may be offered, regardless of whether they are close to home or for the benefit of others. Truth be told, it's regular in a few conventions to use customs to encompass not only thoughts of those within the coven, but also for those outside of it.

In numerous celebrations, a service known as "cakes and brew" (or "cakes and wine") is an imperative part of Wiccan history. Sustenance and drink are offered and emblematically imparted to the God and Goddess, ordinarily toward the end of the ritual.

Wicca: book(s) of shadows

A Book of Shadows is fairly similar to a diary, however with an unequivocally otherworldly and supernatural core interest. It might incorporate spells, names, and dates of Sabbats and Esbats, mantras and other custom dialect, arrangements of enchanted correspondences for hues, precious stones, and herbs, and a large group of another valuable supernatural randomness.

The Book of Shadows is basically a cutting-edge grimoire—a term utilized in the nineteenth century to portray writings covering different Witchcraft activities, for example, enchanted hypothesis, portrayals of ceremonies, guidance in spell work and divination frameworks, magical rationalities, and other exclusive data. Instances of grimoires can be found all through the Middle Ages and much prior, at least going back to stone tablets found in old Egypt and Mesopotamia.

It was Gerald Gardner who received the expression "Book of Shadows" as a title for his very own coven's grimoire, which was intended to be kept a mystery from everyone except the chosen individuals from his coven. The material was added to and updated as time went on, with the understanding that these practices ought not to wind up static and settled, but rather ought to rather stay dynamic, with new ages of Witches including and subtracting from them as they saw fit.

As Witchcraft developed into Wicca, it moved into new and different customs gaining new insight adding to the making of new Book(s) of Shadows – However, not all Wiccans keep a Book(s) of Shadows to record their mystical knowledge and magical experiences. Most covens that abide by the old Wicca traditions keep their mystical knowledge and magical experiences a mystery.

Despite the fact that it is unexpected for a Wiccan to completely share with others their Book of Shadows, it is for that reason that knowledge about it has come into the public domain and gained interest from people. In the current day of the Internet, some Wiccan practitioners actually share their

Book of Shadows online. Therefore, the mystery that surrounds Wicca continues to diminish. However, it is important to note that it is quite standard for Wiccans to conceal their Book of Shadows from other people who might not understand the Craft.

The elements and grounding techniques

Wiccans believe that everything, essentially, comes down to the four elements of earth, air, fire, and water. These elements make up the world, the universe, and ourselves. This connection between us and the elements of the universe is the backbone of Wiccan magick and the theory of how it works.

There is a story not of Wiccan but of Taoist origins which represents this perfectly.

The story tells of an old man who was walking by a river when, suddenly, they lost their balance and fell into the rushing waters. An onlooker, concerned that the old man would drown, sent his proteges to go save the man. But, by the time they reached him, the old man had already washed up on the side of the river and seemed to be undeterred.

When asked how he was able to escape the raging waters, the old man explained that he escaped them by not fighting them. Fighting them meant that he was separate from the river. Instead, he allowed the river to carry him and he became the river. In so doing, he was freed.

Magic has often been labeled as 'supernatural' but Wiccans believe their form of Magick is perfectly natural. They are simply working with nature rather than fighting against it and, in doing so, are able to work what to others may seem like miracles.

To harmonize with the elements and make magick possible, there are a few grounding techniques. However, before we get to them, you can also learn to harmonize with the four elements by trying to adopt their properties into your everyday life.

Earth represents fertility and stability. You can learn to adopt the traits of the Earth by allowing the things you do in life to grow and blossom without having the need to control. And, you can stabilize yourself by learning how to create within you an inner calm and choosing to help people in times you would rather stay far away.

Because fertility takes trust, you must learn to trust the universe. And, because stability requires self-reliance, and it welcomes the people in harder times to seek you out. Let them know you are there for them and your stability with shine, like the rock solid stability of the Earth shines.

Air is connected to the center of your essence but also to the nature of the world. It represents the lightness of your inner spirit but also the winds of change which bring both good and bad things and yet do not have prejudice against them.

You can learn to adopt these traits by being playful and becoming less attached to the world as you know it. These traits come in unison. The inability to be playful stems from taking life too seriously and taking life too seriously is how we try to control the uncontrollable world around us. By loosening up, having fun, and letting life take you where it will, you are welcoming the aspects of air into your being.

Fire is related to vast energy and strong power of will. You can incorporate these traits by dividing your energy more wisely and by staying firm on the things you believe in. In order to do either of these, you must know yourself better than you do currently.

We waste so much time on the things that do not matter and on the trivial. When we choose instead to devote our time and energy to the things important to us, almost limitless energy is born. And, with that energy, we can stay steady and firm on the things we believe in. We can push through the hard days and be a formidable force.

Fire can both create and destroy, so use the energy and willpower it grows within you to do great good, because nothing burns worse than the fire of the universe coming back to haunt you later on. Know yourself and stand strong, but have mercy.

Water is associated with cleansing, passion, and emotion. But the passion represented by water is not a burning passion, but a steady passion. Like the waves which work away at the rock slow and steady, never ceasing, rather than the TNT that could blow the rock away.

In order to allow these traits into your being, you must start with cleansing. By far, the most unclean part of ourselves is the mirror through which we view ourselves. The opinions of others and happenings of the past cloud our opinion of ourselves and often make us increasingly arrogant or devastatingly insecure – both of which are really the same issue expressing themselves in different ways.

To cleanse your inner mirror, you must learn to forgive yourself and let go of the past. Once you have done this, you will see the person you truly are and you will be able to see the clouded images others present – and you will be able to assist them to love themselves as well.

To express the passion of water, you must remain steady and consistent. Passion is not the explosion followed by the silence, but it is the constant working away at your goals. Set something up in your life that seems difficult and work away at it steadily – soon you will know the passion of water.

And, lastly, there is emotion. A word which carries a negative connotation for most people because they rarely see it expressed in any way other than in a burst. So many of us hold in our emotions that, by the time we have a chance to be sad we are devastated or depression, by the time we have a chance to be angry we go on rages or become destructive, by the time we have a chance to express joy it becomes utter mania.

To align with the emotional side of water and allow yourself to harmonize with nature, you must learn to acknowledge what you are feeling and begin to experience emotions in the same way you would experience smells and tastes. You cannot deny them, can you? They certainly are there, you cannot ignore them. But the only time a smell becomes pungent is when the cause has been allowed to fester. Do not allow your emotions to fester, allow them to flow – like water.

When you have become aligned with these elements in the ways outlined, it may not even be necessary to become grounded because you will already be in harmony with the world and the universe. But, until then, grounding will be the only way you can truly take part in magickal practice. Any magickal practice.

Quick Grounding Technique

For quick grounding, you can simple relax yourself in an environment where you are not going to be interrupted. Take slow breaths and try to become aware of what is around you. This works especially well in nature, where you can specifically focus on the earth, air, fire, or water elements depending on your surroundings. The idea is to slow down your mind and body and to reconnect with the world around you. This can be done at any time. It begins when you choose and it ends when you feel stable and relaxed.

Deep Grounding Technique

For deep grounding, you will want to envision far more and settle yourself deep within the visualization. What exactly you envision depends on the technique, but the following is an example:

Place your feet flat on the earth (bare if possible) and keep your back straight. Relax your mind, relax your body. Breath slow.

Now, imagine the earth beneath your feet. Envision the layers of soil or flooring beneath you, way, way down. The further down you can see the better. Then, imagine a golden snake of energy slithering up through the layers, one by one, until finally it enters through your feet.

Feel the golden energy spread down to your toes and then up your legs, your back and fill up your stomach. Imagine it shining on your heart and passing into your arms and neck. And finally, feel the golden light's warmth as it spreads through your face and up through the crown of your head. Imagine the golden snake reaching high to the sky.

Focus on the warmth and the stillness of your being for a few moments before reversing direction, slowly, from the sky down through your body, out of your feet and back down deep in the Earth. Imagine the golden light leaving you gradually from head to toe.

You have now been grounded, thoroughly, and may continue on with magickal practice or with the rest of your day.

Chapter 10 Simple Spells and Rituals

- Casting a Circle

A magickal circle is multifunctional. It carves out sacred space, keeps wanted energy in, and keeps unwanted energy out. Sacred space is traditionally a place between worlds and dimensions. It's a section of time and space that does not belong to the mundane, nor is it completely etheric. It is where magickal rites and rituals are performed: "a time that is not a time and place that is not a place; between the worlds and beyond". It serves a temple that can be erected anywhere.

As a beginner, it's advisable to cast a circle prior to all forms of magickal practice and worship. Simply casting a circle to sit and meditate or to bond with the God and Goddess is perfectly acceptable. Practicing magick is of course just that—a practice. Witches and Magicians are practitioners of magick just as doctors are practitioners of medicine. The only way to become adept is through practice and experience.

The more times you cast a circle, the more familiar you will become with the ritual and with your own ritual mindset. Getting to know yourself in the circle is one the most effective forms of refining your Craft. Eventually, some Witches find that casting a circle is only necessary when performing major magickal workings, while others may continue to cast a circle before all spiritual work including their morning meditation.

The best advice is to do what feels right for you. There is no "wrong way" in Wicca. It's all about finding what works best for you as an individual—this is how your magick becomes effective. Trial and error are necessary within a magickal practice.

With that in mind, note that the following steps are only guidelines. This is one of the simplest ways to cast a circle. Some methods are more formal, and require several other steps. Feel free to omit, modify, or add whatever resonates with you and makes you feel the most comfortable.

1. Cleanse and Purify the Ritual Space

Traditionally, the room or area is cleaned. Physically cleaning begins the process of clearing out any stale or negative energy. If you're inside, this means picking up strewn items, sweeping or vacuuming, etc. If you're outside, clear away branches and debris. In some Wiccan traditions, the floors and walls are always scrubbed before casting a circle. If you're a solitary eclectic practitioner, you can take the cleaning as far as is comfortable for you personally.

If you're in a place that doesn't allow for this step, that's fine as well. However, you definitely want to energetically cleanse the space. Smudging with sage, sprinkling salt water, fanning incense around the area, playing a musical instrument or singing bowls will neutralize the environment. You can simultaneously visualize a white light filling the room and pushing out any negativity that may be present.

2. Set Up

An altar is ideally located in the middle of the room, facing either north or east. Again, if this is impractical, you can still cast a circle with your altar against a wall or in corner through visualization. The idea is for your altar or working space to be in the middle of the circle.

-       Make sure you have everything you'll need for the spellwork. Once the circle is cast, if you need to leave the circle for any reason, "cutting" a door with your athame or wand is customary.

-       Lay out your altar cloth and arrange your tools.

-       Determine how large your circle needs to be to accommodate the type of work you will performing. Most solitary practitioners can work comfortably in circle with a six-foot radius. Others may require less or more.

-       If possible, mark the ground to visibly show where your circle will be. This could be done by laying a rope or cord of some kind in a circle, a chalk outline, a ring of salt, flowers laid stem to petals, or simply four candles placed at the cardinal points of your circle. If you're working up against walls, you can visualize the boundaries of the circle through the wall.

-       Light your working candles.

3. Cast the Circle

There are a number of ways to do this. The simplest way is as follows:

- Begin by standing at the north end of your circle's outline with athame or wand in hand. If you're using only your hand, extend your pointer and middle finger to assist in the projection of your energy.

- Point your tool towards the ground where your circle will begin, and visualize a stiff beam of protective energy being directed into the ground. This energy is coming from you, and is only being directed into the ground by the athame or wand.

- Walk clockwise (also known as "deosil") around your circle, while continuing to project the beam of protective energy into the ground. The stronger your visualization, the stronger your circle will be. Take your time, and don't rush through the casting.

- Once you return to the north, your circle is complete.

4. Grounding and Centering

Once your circle is cast, take a few moments to sit at your altar space and take several deep breaths. Light some incense of your choice, and meditate for however long it takes to enter a ritual mindset. Commune with the God and Goddess. Invite any deities to come and witness your rites. You will notice a shift in your consciousness. When you do, it's time to begin your magickal work.

5. Perform Any Magickal Work

After casting the circle and entering the ritual mindset, it's time to perform your spell, or complete whatever magickal task you set out to accomplish.

6. Close the Circle

When you've cast your spell or otherwise completed your magickal work, you might want to stand up and thank the Goddess and God for attending. After doing so, you can begin closing the circle.

- Stand at the north point of the circle with your athame, wand, or fingers pointed toward the ground.

- Visualize the beam of protective energy retracting back up into you.

- Walk counterclockwise (also known as "widdershins") around the circle, while continuing to visualize the beam being retracted.

- Once you reach north, the circle is closed.

7. "Cakes and Ale"

After all your spiritual work is complete, you may want to sip and nibble on some treats to reintroduce yourself to the mundane world.

Simple Candle Spell to Manifest Love

This spell can be adapted to manifest love of all kinds. Simply alter the color of the candle, the herbs and oils used (if any), and the intention to reflect what you want to attract.

1. Define Your Intention

First, there must be an intention. What would you like to accomplish with the spell? As an example, let's say you'd like to work on self-love and invite a loving relationship with yourself. From what we've already learned, we know that this is a form of creation magick—you want to bring something in.

What would this intention look and feel like to you? Imagine yourself bubbling with happiness, feeling loved and accepted. Maybe imagine yourself having a conversation with someone else and feeling confident. Keep this image in your mind and really feel the emotions associated with it throughout the entire spellcasting process.

2. Timing: Determine When to Cast the Spell

Choosing when to cast is dependent on each individual spell. Since this spell is going to invite self-love into your life, you would want to work with the Goddess and attune your spell to the waxing phase of the moon (the full moon would also promote this and all other spells).

To clarify how we came to this conclusion of when to cast, let's say you are casting a spell to smoothly end a relationship with someone else instead. Rather than cast the spell during the waxing phase of the moon when the energy is best suited for building, the waning phase would be more appropriate since the waning moon represents ebbing or subsiding.

Timing a spell can include many more factors: the day of the week, month of the year, and the astrological placement of other planets. However, as a beginner, timing your simple candle magick spell with the corresponding phase of the moon is a great way to start.

3. Select a Candle: Color and Size

Next, you will need to choose a candle best-suited to your intention. Below you will find a list of colors and their correspondences. For this example, spell, you are inviting self-love into your life, so you may feel drawn to use either a pink candle or a red candle. Traditionally, pink symbolizes a soft, sentimental love—charming and sweet.

In addition to self-love, pink is also commonly used for friendships, familial connections, healing, femininity, and the more romantic aspects of a lover-to-lover relationship. However, if red feels more like love to you, or if any other color better symbolizes the type of love you're wanting to attract, please use that color. In spellwork there are only guidelines. The most potent spells are custom-made.

In addition to the color of the candle, the shape and size are also dependent on the individual spell. Generally, votive and tapers are sufficient for almost any spell. You will find that votive and tapers are readily available in an assortment of colors. Large, seven-day candles are appropriate for more intensive work, as these will burn continuously for a week. For our sample spell, a pink votive or taper would be ideal.

Below is a list of the most commonly used colors and some of their correspondences. These will vary depending on the Witch. Follow your intuition. For example, if a gold candle feels more like prosperity to you than a green candle, then use a gold candle for your prosperity work.

- White

White candles can be used in place of any other color. If you need a pink candle but only have white on hand, the white candle will do just fine. As you may know, this logic comes from the field of physics. It has been scientifically observed that white is all colors. What we see as white is actually all the wavelengths of visible light at once—all the colors in the spectrum.

Common correspondences of white include: healing, protection, the Goddess, purity, enlightenment, etc.

- Black

Just as white is all colors, black is the absence of color.

Correspondences: banishing, reversals, protection, pure potential, the blank canvas.

- Green

Many thinks of the lush, fertile Earth during spring and summer.

Correspondences: the element of Earth, the heart chakra. abundance, prosperity, money, career, the material world, etc.

- Pink

Correspondences: romance, self-love, friendship, partnerships, the planet Venus, femininity, etc.

- Red

- Correspondences: the element of fire, the root chakra, passion, lust, desire, ambition, courage, strength, power, renewal, transformation etc.

- *Purple or Violet*

Correspondences: the element of spirit, clairvoyance, psychic abilities, meditation, third eye, wisdom, spiritual protection, etc.

- Blue

Correspondences: the element of water, the throat chakra, calming, healing, truth, justice, etc.

- Orange

Correspondences: the element of fire, the root chakra, cleansing, refreshing, motivation, ambition, optimism, activity, warmth, welcoming, etc.

- Yellow

Correspondences: the element of air, the solar plexus chakra, clarity, sunlight, cheery, communication, words, sound, intellect, logic, etc.

- Brown

Correspondences: the element of earth, stability, domestic life, animals/pets, material goods, physical health, etc.

4. Cast a Circle (optional)

The previous three steps were preparation. Now is the time to cast your circle, if you feel compelled to do so, and begin your work.

5. Dress the Candle (optional)

Many Witches feel that dressing a candle adds to the potency of the spell. Dressing a candle refers to carving letters, symbols, and/or sigils into the candle, followed by coating the candle with essential oils and herbs which resonate with the intention of the spell. In the following section titled, "Herbal Magick", you will find a list of commonly used herbs and their correspondences.

For our example spell of inviting love, you may want to dress your pink votive or taper by carving a few hearts into it, anointing it with rose oil, and rolling it in rosemary and/or jasmine. The process of dressing a candle is generally done as follows:

-     Carving the Candle

Choose a symbol which is meaningful for you and corresponds to the intention of the spell. Carve the symbol into the candle where ever and however many times you see fit. You can be as elaborate and detailed as you want with the etchings, or simple and rudimentary.

In any case, be sure that you are focusing on your intention throughout the entire carving process. You can even imagine your desire being transferred into the candle through the markings. Any tools can be used for the carving—safety pin, needle, pencil, etc. Some Witches will only use their athame, and that's fine as well.

-     Anointing the Candle with Oil

Apply two or three drops of the oil into the palm of your hand. Then, clutch the candle in your hand while still thinking of your intention. Massage the oil (and your intention) into the candle. Please note that if you don't have a specific oil for a spell available, like rose oil, you can always make your own in a pinch.

If you have roses nearby, take a few petals and put them in a container with some olive oil or whatever oil you have on hand. Don't be afraid to improvise when necessary. Remember, you are what makes the spell work.

- Rolling the Candle in Herbs

Once the candle is anointed with your desired oil, you will lay the candle on a bed of your chosen herbs. Since our example spell is to bring something into your life, rolling the candle toward you is fitting. Contrarily, if you were performing a spell to rid something from your life, rolling the candle away from you to coat it with herbs would be preferable.

6. Light the Candle and Raise Energy

When you feel that the candle is ready to be lit, take a few deep breaths and place the candle in a holder of your choosing. You can use a lighter, matches, whatever feels most comfortable. Take some time to sit and meditate with the flame. Soften your gaze, let your lids droop a bit. Use the flame as a focal point for visualizing your intention.

You can continue to visualize and feel the emotions of the scenes you've chosen. Additionally, chanting and swaying or rocking helps to raise the energy. You can begin by swaying back and forth slowly and gradually you will pick up speed. Chants don't have to rhyme unless you prefer them to.

If you're drawn to chanting, you can simply say whatever is in your heart to describe your intention. As an example, for this spell you might want to chant something straightforward like, "I love myself unconditionally". Alternatively, you can compose a beautiful piece of poetry to recite. Again, do what feels natural.

7. Disposal

Customarily, the candle is left to burn out on its own. The purpose of allowing the candle to self-extinguish is two-fold. Firstly, as the candle burns, it is releasing your intention and all that energy you imbued it with into the universe through the flame and the rising heat. Secondly, each time you see the candle burning, you are reminded of the spell and your intention.

This second aspect of the manifestation has a continuous impact on the subconscious mind. Meaning, you may not always consciously acknowledge your spellwork when you pass by the candle, but it does have a subconscious impact each and every time.

8. Close the Circle (optional)

If you casted a circle before beginning your work, now is the time to commence with closing.

Simple Candle Spell to Banish

This spell primarily utilizes the fire element to rid yourself of something unwanted. Fire is swift and thorough in its transformation. The results will manifest quickly, but the route of manifestation can be situationally intense.

1. Define Your Intention

What needs to be banished from your life with urgency? This could be something like a stalker, or another type of threatening presence in your life. You may want to quickly end an abusive relationship or legal situation.

2. Time Your Work

If possible, it would be ideal to wait until the time of the dark moon to perform an abrupt banishing. Perhaps the dark moon is within a few days. If not, the next most appropriate time would be during the full moon, or the waning moon.

3. Select a Candle: Color and Size

A black votive or taper candle is ideal for banishing. Black corresponds to the dark moon and the energy of renewal.

4. Cast a Circle (optional)

Cast your circle in preparation for your spellwork.

5. Write Down What You Want to Banish

On a small slip of paper, write down what you want to banish. While you're writing, be sure to focus on your intention. Visualize the situation being released and feel the emotions associated with it. Channel it all onto the slip of paper through your pen.

6. Dress the Candle (optional)

You might feel drawn to carve the candle with corresponding symbols or words. Carving what you wrote on the slip of paper works well. You can also dress your candle with the appropriate oils and herbs as detailed in the previous spell. For banishing, try anointing your candle with clove oil and coating it with crushed bay leaves by rolling it away from you.

7. Light the Candle and Burn the Slip of Paper

Light your black candle, which represents the transformative element of fire. The slip of paper is now representative of the situation or person you'd like to banish from your life. Hold the paper over the candle's flame and allow it to ignite. Once it's smoldering well, drop it into your cauldron or other fire-safe receptacle. Let it burn to ash. Continue to visualize the situation and emotions being released.

8. Close the Circle (optional)

You may want to close the circle at this time.

9. Disposal

Allow your black candle to burn down completely. The ashes can be disposed of by way of any other element. Toss them into the wind, bury them in the ground, flush them down the toilet, or throw them into a running body of water.

Create with the Earth Element: Simple Flower Spell

The element of Earth is solid, steady, and gradual in its pace. Think of how slowly but perfectly a tree grows—this **is** Earth magick. The intricacies of constructing a tree take time to complete. Thus, any intention that you cast utilizing the Earth element will manifest into your world much like the evolution of a tree. It will take ample amounts of time to flourish, but the results will be long-lasting, sturdy and well-composed. Consider manifesting with the element of Earth when your intention would most benefit from "slow and steady wins the race".

The concept of the flower spell is to charge a seed with your desire and then plant it. As the flower buds and blooms under your care, so will your desire bloom into your physical world.

1. Define Your Intention

This spell is for something you'd like to bring into your life (or generally bring into being) gradually and smoothly. It will be something you want to carefully nurture into fruition. Perhaps you are repairing a relationship with a certain individual; trust may have been breached, but you're both ready to rebuild.

This takes time and patience, which is in perfect alignment with the element of Earth. Alternatively, you may want to foster peace and bring more love to the world. Perhaps you want to become pregnant and grow a healthy child. These are all prime examples of intentions that are best manifested through the element of earth.

2. Timing

Since you are wanting to gradually cultivate something, you will want to correlate your spell with the waxing phase of the moon.

3. Charge the Seeds

You can select a specific type of seed that correlates with your intention or has some significance—rose, sunflower, carnation. Cup the seeds in your hand and concentrate on your intention. This time it will be the seeds that are representing your desire.

Focus on the emotions associated with what you want to bring forth. If you're casting this spell for fertility, visualize the healthy development of your baby within the womb, and then visualize rocking him or her in your arms. Feel the emotions as if the event is presently taking place. Visualize these emotions and images being transferred into the seeds.

4. Plant the Seeds

Once you feel that you've sufficiently raised and transferred the energy, it's time to plant the seeds. You can plant them in your backyard, directly into the earth. If this is not possible, a large pot or container filled with fertile soil is just fine. Wherever you plant the seeds, make sure they are accessible to the sun's nourishing rays.

5. Cultivate

Nurture your seeds into buds and beyond. Water them, talk to them, give them love. As your flower grows and blooms, so will your intention.

Banish with the Earth Element: Simple Apple Spell

This spell imbues an apple with something you want to banish. Then, by burying the charged apple in the ground, you rid yourself of the unwanted aspect gradually and organically.

1. Define Your Intention

You realize there is something you want to remove from your reality. Reflecting on the issue, you decide that this aspect of your life would best be dissolved gradually and delicately, rather than instantly go up in flames or get turbulently washed away in torrent. Some examples might be: gracefully ending a relationship with someone, banishing bad habits, addictions, weight, negative thought patterns, emotional blocks, hate or racism on the planet.

By invoking the element of Earth to gradually and sustainably banish these aspects, you are ensuring the durability of the results. You won't successfully crash diet, for example, and then gain all the weight back shortly after. Rather, you may start taking real steps toward a complete lifestyle change instead. The results will not be instantaneous like working with the fire element, but they will be more likely to last.

2. Time Your Work

Since you are gradually banishing, you will want to time your spell with the waning phase of the moon.

3. Cast a Circle (optional)

4. Charge the Apple

Select an apple or any other fruit with thin skin. You're going to charge the apple with your intention just as you would with a candle. Hold the apple in your hands and focus on what you want to remove from your world. Really feel all the associated emotions and transfer them to the apple.

If you're wanting to banish an addiction like smoking, for example, feel that craving for nicotine, feel the guilt every time you light up, feel the burn in your throat, feel the toxins flooding your body, feel the tightness in your chest, and send all those sensations and emotions into the apple.

You'll notice that the apple now represents your addiction, just like the candle represented your desire in the candle magick spell for self-love. No matter what you're wanting to banish, the apple will **become** that thing once it is charged with the energy of that thing. In other words, the apple simply becomes another medium for your thoughtforms to be physically manipulated.

You can get as elaborate as you'd like with charging the apple. Consider carving the apple with symbols just as you would carve a candle. Cutting the apple in half, spooning out the core, and then filling it with tobacco or cigarette butts is a more tangible way of imprinting your intention to quit smoking. You can also fill and/or dress the apple with any oils or herbs you feel are conducive. Additionally, you may want to include chants in the process of charging or burying.

5. Bury the Apple

You'll recall that candle magick primarily utilized the element of fire. Once the candle was charged with your intention, you lit the candle and let it burn away. Instead of burning the charged apple, you will bury it deep in the ground—this principally employs the element of earth rather than fire.

As the apple slowly and permanently decomposes from your reality, so will whatever you wish to banish. It will be absorbed back into the earth, and the energy dispersed away from your life.

Conclusion

Moon energy is just one kind of energy. It is potent and readily available any night of the year. Even during the new Moon, there is a kind of lunar energy to be had.

But lunar energy is not required to perform magic. You can perform spells that run counter to the Moon's energy if you call upon the Watchtowers, spirits, or even your ancestors. The Moon is powerful but it does not dictate everything.

And this is part of the balance that sits at the core of Wicca. In order to fully work with Moon magic, you must understand its benefits and limitations. Magic, like any other tool, is guided by both.

And as you explore various branches of magic, you will find one that works best for you. This can only happen when you've taken the time to fully understand each branch you've explored.

If Moon magic is where you find your magical home, embrace it. Bolster your spells with images of the Moon, songs in Her honor, and representations of all the Moon's phases. Call upon all aspects of the goddess and learn to walk in the shadows that fall when it is the dark of the Moon.

You may also find that studying Moon magic leads you as much to astronomy as astrology. Do not fight this pull. Understanding the Moon and the celestial bodies that move around it will only serve to enhance your power. In your studies you will find that Moon magic intersects with other branches of celestial magic, such as star magic and Sun magic. Go where your studies leads you.

Learn and grow within the Moon's light. She is always ready to guide you.

CPSIA information can be obtained
at www.ICGtesting.com
Printed in the USA
BVHW011947201220
596137BV00016B/401

9 781801 257275